T0209610

Lust for Life

Lust for Life

On the Writings of Kathy Acker

Edited by Amy Scholder, Carla Harryman, and Avital Ronell

VERSO

First published by Verso 2006
© in the collection Verso 2006
© in the contributions, the individual contributors
All rights reserved

The moral rights of the authors and editors have been asserted

1 3 5 7 9 10 8 6 4 2

Verso
UK: 6 Meard Street, London W1F 0EG
USA: 388 Atlantic Ave, Brooklyn, NY 11217
www.versobooks.com

Verso is the imprint of New Left Books

ISBN 978-1-84467-066-6

British Library Cataloguing in Publication Data
A catalogue record for this book is available from the British Library

Library of Congress Cataloging-in-Publication Data
A catalog record for this book is available from the Library of Congress

Typeset in Garamond by
Hewer Text UK Ltd, Edinburgh
Printed in the United States

Contents

Preface

On November 7, 2002, almost exactly five years after Kathy Acker died of cancer at the age of fifty, an illustrious group of scholars, writers, artists, playwrights and rock stars got together for a two-day event at the Fales Library at New York University to discuss and examine and read her work.

The purpose of the symposium was not to memorialize, though there were many friends, colleagues, and long-time readers still in mourning. Rather, we were there to study and attend to a body of work that has had significant influence on late twentieth-century cultural practice. We were all aware of the fact that, in her lifetime, Acker enjoyed too little of the recognition her work deserved. But this gathering did not depend for its passionate unfolding on Acker's absence; in fact, we all wished she could have been there to defend, argue with, and disrupt the proceedings.

I organized the symposium with Marvin Taylor, the Director of Fales Library & Special Collections at NYU, Carla Harryman and Avital Ronell. It included these speakers: David Antin, Caroline Bergvall, Nayland Blake, Leslie Dick, Richard Foreman, Ellen Friedman, Diamanda Galas, Robert Glück, Kim Gordon, Judith Halberstam, Kathleen Hanna, Carla Harryman, Susan Hawkins, Linda Kauffman, Eleanor Kaufman, Chris Kocela, Liz Kotz, Catherine Liu, Rick Moody, Avital Ronell, Sapphire, Leslie Scalapino, Carolee Schneemann, Sarah Schulman, Eve Sedgwick, Chris Tysh, Matias Viegener, Barrett Watten, and Peter Wollen.

Kathy Acker got attention for her arresting image, relentless outsider status, and provocative reading style, which often directed new readers to her published works. Once she died, she lost that entrée into new audiences. I became concerned that her work—which has been so vitally informative for a young constituency in desperate need of as deeply radical a figure as Kathy Acker—would become obscure.

When a writer is no longer around to produce new works, the oeuvre either takes on a life of its own, or it fades away. But neither outcome just happens. In order for an oeuvre to take on a life of its own, communities of readers must continually re-establish its relevance and power, and through these interactions and discussions and references and arguments the work thrives, summoning an essence of the vitality and scandal in which it originated.

The gathering at NYU in 2002—with over 1000 people in attendance—was a strong indication that Acker's work would survive its author. At the same time, I put together two posthumous Kathy Acker books: one consisting of two early Acker works, *Rip-Off Red, Girl Detective* and *The Burning Bombing of America: The Destruction of the US*; the other, which I co-edited with Dennis Cooper, called *Essential Acker: The Selected Writings of Kathy Acker*, with an introduction by Jeanette Winterson (both published by Grove Press). The fact that Acker's twelve major publications remain in print to this day is also promising, but I don't take it for granted.

This volume, published almost ten years after Acker's death, indicates a new level of inquiry and scholarship into Acker's literary project. It was inspired by the talks given at the NYU symposium in 2002, and also makes clear the breadth and interdisciplinary reach of Acker and of those who read and write about her.

The sophistication, prescience, and innovation of Acker's work make it prime material for scholarly interpretation and academic study. My hope is that with this collection of essays, we set the stage for further inquiry into Acker's project, and that general readers, students, and scholars take note of the myriad ways to penetrate and interact with this vibrant work.

I produced this volume with Carla Harryman and Avital Ronell. I am very grateful to them for their collaboration and wisdom.

Amy Scholder
November 2005

Kathy Acker

Peter Wollen

Writing about Goya's "Black Paintings" in *Art After Modernism*, a 1984 collection of essays published by the New Museum in downtown New York, Kathy Acker drew the conclusion, "The only reaction against an unbearable society is equally unbearable nonsense." She once said she didn't expect anyone to read all the way through any of her books from beginning to end—"even in *Empire of the Senseless*, which is the most narrative book, you could read pretty much anywhere," or, in other words, you could make your own montage, you could appropriate and re-order, just as Kathy Acker had appropriated and re-ordered the writing of others—Harold Robbins or Cervantes or Ian Fleming or Propertius. Leslie Dick once remarked that Kathy Acker's writing was an extension of her reading, that her plagiarism was a way of reading, or re-reading, appropriating and customizing what she read, writing herself, so to speak, into the fabric of the original text. Acker used to read her own texts too, each one eight times, re-drafting it after each reading—once for meaning, once for beauty, once for sound, once to the mirror to see how it looked, once for rhythm, once for structure, and so on. Writing and reading became as confused and mixed up together as sense and nonsense, as male and female, as self and other, as the sexual and the political. Writing about Caravaggio's *David with the Head of Goliath*, Kathy Acker commented on its nihilism, as she saw it: "The sexual is the political realm. There is no engagement."

Barbara Kruger paid outrageous homage to Acker by rewriting, or rather parodying her work that same year in the New York art journal, *ZG*. To Kruger, herself well known for her appropriation of pre-existing images, Kathy Acker's writing seemed that of a nihilist, rather than a critic. No engagement. Nonsense. Nothing. "Your quick-change artistry is a crafty dance of guises, cover-ups for that which you know best; nothing. And all the books, sex, movies, charm bracelets, and dope in the world can't cover up this nothing. And you know this very well since you are a librarian, a whore, a director, a jeweler, and a dealer." In the end, it all boils down to baby talk, to unbearable nonsense: "Goo goo." It is more complex than that. Kathy Acker drew on an extraordinarily wide range of sources and a very complex methodology of writing in order, not so much to express herself as to dissolve herself into a torrent of textuality. This is far from nihilism or nothingness, even if it constantly rejected being for becoming. She was a ceaseless explorer of the disorienting potential of language, its directness, its capacity to drag the reader right into the text, "because that's the only way you can take the journey." Acker's work, more than that of any other writer I can think of, challenged the traditional lines of demarcation between poetry and novel, between high culture and popular trash, and, perhaps most important of all, between literature and art world. In all these respects, her work signalled the tremors of a deep cultural shift, as she sought to negotiate a new relationship between avant-garde artist and popular entertainer, between esoterica and pulp, between conceptualism and narrative.

"Bookworm parrot Legba biker orphan pirate poet." Like Kruger, when I once jotted down a kind of parodic capsule version of Acker's work, I began with the love of books, with the ceaseless consumption of books. Parrot of course goes with pirate—parroting texts, pirating texts, two ways of speaking about plagiarism, or appropriation, as it is more discreetly known. *Détournement*, perhaps, to use the situationist term, or re-functioning, to use Brecht's, re-functioning by re-contextualizing, by making strange. Parrot also meant lovebird for Kathy Acker. Commissioned by the American Opera Projects of New York, for a production in spring 1998, Acker returned once again to her childhood. In a New York City hospital, a mother, Claire (Mrs Alexander), her daughter, Electra, and her mother's best friend Betsy are all gathered together. Betsy is even richer than Claire, but wears a thrift-store dress and colorless stockings so as not to appear "nouveau riche." Electra, picking her lips, slouches down in her chair, trying to be invisible while eavesdropping on a sailor or, better still, a pirate. Pirates are outlaws, too. They go with bikers, the wild ones, the rebels. But Acker's rebels always had a cause—art always went together with politics, writing was a way of subverting the words of the parents, the authorized version, the authoritarian text. Like Burroughs said, it was a way of destroying the word-lines, storming the reality studio. It was a way of escaping the double binds imposed by the structures of family and society—sexual, textual, ontological. Who am I? What is the meaning of "I"? What kind of a word is that, what kind of a trickster?

When Kathy Acker died, I was depressed by much of the obituary coverage in the newspapers. I could not help remembering what she had said about England when she talked with Sylvère Lotringer: "In England it was absolutely horrible . . . the media image is so much this kind of sexual image. I'm very well known there and I get tons of work, but to say that they like what I do, no, I wouldn't say that. They fetishize what I do." She had become an object of *virtù*, or perhaps I should say, of vice. She was seen as a fascinating and mysterious icon, an agent provocateur sent from some alien realm. I remembered something else she had said too: "I've always hated the English view of the novel . . . that there should be irony . . . distance . . . a very fine cool style, a very conservative way of writing a novel." I was glad when I found Diamanda Galas's tribute on the internet—"I once had a conversation with her late one night in Switzerland, and I was astonished to discover not only a provocateur but an extremely rigorous thinker with an encyclopedic knowledge of her craft." Galas identified her as "a keeper of the flame of our blood brothers, Nerval and Artaud and Baudelaire." She ended by quoting, in farewell, a stanza of Baudelaire about a sailor setting out on a voyage. It was one dimension of Acker's work—the tale of the damned, the voyager, the outsider—but, even then, it is not the whole story. In some ways, it is very simple to understand where she was coming from.

Kathy Acker's aesthetic and political stance (once again, it is hard to separate the two) was set for life in San Diego, where she went as a student toward the end of the 1960s. Born and brought up in New York, she had first attended Brandeis University and it was because Herbert Marcuse left Brandeis to become a Professor at UC San Diego that Acker also left to follow him out west to Southern California. Then, in San Diego, she not only continued her academic relationship with Marcuse but she also encountered conceptual art. In fact, very early on, she fell under the aesthetic influence of another mentor who introduced her to the European avant-garde, to Black Mountain poetry and to conceptualism—David Antin, whose interest in conceptual art, as well as his use of improvisation as a mode of literary composition and writing as a performance form, stayed with her through every twist and turn of her career. Talking about Kathy, David Antin once told me about teaching creative writing to students. They felt they should write from their experience of life but he knew they had not really had any experience of life, so he would tell them, "Don't be afraid to *copy it out*," to find it in a book and work with that. "Kathy really took that ball and ran with it," he said. Later she could find a different, deeper rationale for copying it out, for plagiarism (although, as she always argued, it wasn't really plagiarism because she was quite open about what she did).

She was also influenced by Jerome Rothenberg, a poet who was loosely attached to the Beat writers, but whose profounder sympathies were with the European avant-garde, especially French surrealism and German expressionism. Thus the influence of Marcuse, with his radical neo-Freudian emphasis on the role of *eros* in politics converged with an equally radical artistic avant-gardism. Acker was active in the student movement (Students for a Democratic Society) and also worked as a teaching assistant for Marcuse, as did Martha Rosler and Alan Sekula, two fellow students who went on to become prominent radical artists, combining photography, conceptual art, and political militancy, as Acker combined documentary writing with conceptualism and leftist politics. Equally, if not more important, Eleanor Antin (married to David Antin) provided a role model for Acker as a female performer and avant-gardist, one of the first women to make her mark as a conceptual artist. William Burroughs is usually mentioned as the single most important influence on Acker's writing, but, although he was plainly extremely important to her, the context in which she read Burroughs had already been set by the cultural formation that she had received in San Diego.

Talking to Sylvère Lotringer in 1991, Acker commented that "David Antin had been my mentor and had introduced me to the early conceptual artists Dan Graham and Joseph Kosuth" and also that he taught her, "You just don't sit down and write, you have to know why you write and why you use certain methodologies." In this context, she found in Burroughs a prose writer who "was dealing with how politics and language came together . . . Burroughs was the only prose writer I could find who was a conceptualist, oh he's very much of a conceptualist." Burroughs's cut-up technique provided Acker not only with a methodology but also an example of how a literary technique could be given a political twist as a mode of resistance, envisaged as a way of subverting the control system inherent in verbal discourse, expanding the possibilities of writing, ceaselessly creating the new out of the old. Acker went on to describe how she later made use of sections from Burroughs's book *The Third Mind* "as experiments to teach myself how to write." *The Third Mind* was a work produced in collaboration with Brion Gysin, using cut-ups and collages, structured by an elaborate grid system. Created in Paris in the mid-1960s, it was not published until 1978, by which time Acker had returned east to New York. It was not one of the master's more straightforwardly literary works, such as *The Naked Lunch,* which intrigued her the most, but a much more formally extreme and experimental text, composed in concert with Gysin, a visual artist with a background in the Lettrist International, an avant-garde movement whose own roots combined dada and surrealism with an interest in pictography, concrete poetry, and imaginary languages.

Kathy Acker was deeply committed to this avant-garde tradition, a tradition that was much stronger in the visual arts. She used not only cut-up but also incorporated calligraphy, self-drawn dream maps and Persian and Arabic script into her books. She simply added these new techniques to her ongoing concern with experimental writing. In San Francisco, where she lived after her graduate studies were finished, she had distributed her writing in serial form as part of a mail art network, another spin-off from conceptualism, this time in the form of a mode of distribution rather than production, one with its own political spin as the model for a de-centered community, based on reciprocity and a culture of the gift rather than the commodity. She sent her work to anyone who asked for it, free. When she arrived back in New York towards the end of the 1970s, Acker quickly abandoned the world of the St Mark's Poetry Project, her first port of call, for the downtown art world. It turned out that her mail art writings were already known to artists in New York and this, in turn, led to her first true publications, the chapbook editions of her *Black Tarantula* writings and *The Adult Life of Toulouse Lautrec,* with drawings by William Wegman.

Both publications were subsidized by Sol LeWitt, another leading conceptual artist, who had them printed by a small artist's press in association with Printed Matter, the leading outlet for conceptual book art. Acker recalled,

> Sol went to Ted Castle and Leandro Katz—Ted is an art critic and Leandro a filmmaker [while Leandro is indeed a fine experimental filmmaker, he was and is also a gallery artist]—and he said he wanted to print these texts as real books. He basically became my patron. I didn't know who Ted and Leandro were—I thought they were part of the St Mark's poetry scene—so I came back to New York and lo and behold it wasn't that scene at all. They had a party for my book and Joseph Kosuth and Keith Sonnier were there. I was

absolutely flabbergasted 'cause I'd been reading *ArtForum* regularly and worshipped these people. I don't think I could open my mouth all evening [a startling confession on Kathy Acker's part!]. From then on I was just in the art world.

Artists in New York had begun to purloin images—Barbara Kruger, Sherry Levine, Richard Prince, David Salle. Here too Acker found parallels for her own techniques of appropriation. On the Lower East Side others began to cross-hatch avant-gardism with porn, pulp, and schlock, the lower reaches of popular culture, in the birth-pangs of a vernacular postmodernism. This was the milieu of "No Wave," successor to punk, of the Mudd Club, *Raw Magazine*, and underground performance.

Soon she was part of a group of younger artists, peers rather than idols, father figures like Kosuth or LeWitt. She was writing for *Bomb*, *Top Stories*, *Between C & D*, places where artwork and writing by downtown artists was printed alongside writing by downtown writers—Constance De Jong, Gary Indiana, Lynne Tillman. Their enthusiasm underlines how important art-world ideas and practices were to Acker, as she struggled to import a virulent contemporary avant-gardism into the world of literature. Even the poets at St Mark's, considered an avant-garde mecca for modernists, were baffled by her approach to writing. An added difficulty, in their case, came from her insistence on writing prose rather than poetry. Acker's debt to Black Mountain—to Charles Olson, in particular, whose work she had known since she was a schoolgirl—is quite clear, and it is strange that this should somehow have gone unrecognized, at least as she saw it, because she was not considered to be a poet. She adapted his concern with writing as language-driven, with a certain kind of incantatory text, based on the bodily cadence of the breath, while introducing these preoccupations into the writing of prose rather than poetry. Acker's immense debt to Gertrude Stein has also been largely overlooked, perhaps because poets see Stein as a prose writer and novelists see her as a poet. Acker constantly stepped across genre lines (as she did across gender lines) and caused confusion in both camps. The only contemporaneous poets to whom Acker became at all close were the Language Poets, celebrated, though also criticized, by Fredric Jameson—she contributed to their journal $L=A=N=G=U=A=G=E$ and both collaborated with and borrowed from the leading woman exponent of the school, Carla Harryman. In England, she made contact with Michael Horovitz, advocate both for avant-garde poetry and live performance.

In *The Transformation of the Avant-Garde*, dealing with the history of the New York art world from 1940 to 1985, Sarah Crane points out that because novels sell at a much lower price than paintings or other artworks, the market for literature is therefore much greater and commercial success comes from volume of sales. For visual artists, on the other hand, it comes from selling, for a high unit price, to an elite of collectors and museums who are guided in their opinions and tastes by currents they pick up from within the art world itself. As a result, rich and successful artists are often militantly avant-garde in their commitments or their general approach, whereas best-selling writers tend to write "in the tradition of the realistic novel" and avant-garde writers cannot realistically hope for much commercial success. When it does come, as it did, to some extent, in Kathy Acker's case, it is because of the content rather than the form. Gertrude Stein was commercially successful with *The Autobiography of Alice B. Toklas* largely because of its vivid pen-portraits of celebrities from the art world, rather than because of her own experimental writings, even though these were inspired, to a considerable extent, by those very same artists. Virginia Woolf became famous and successful long after her death because of public fascination with the Bloomsbury lifestyle and because of the attention paid to women writers by the women's movement. Joyce, Lawrence, and Burroughs all had to undergo legal prosecution for their works before notoriety could be translated into celebrity, marginality into the mainstream.

For novelists, inevitably, the art world became a model of avant-garde possibility. All of the writers I mentioned, it goes without saying, had close connections with the art world. Stein was both a collector and close friend of Matisse and Picasso. Woolf's circle was directly responsible for the launch of Matisse and Picasso in England, as well as the beginnings of abstraction in British art itself. Joyce's supporters in Paris, Crosby and Jolas, saw his work primarily in the context of Picasso and Brancusi, dada and surrealism. Wyndham Lewis became better known as an artist than as a novelist. Lawrence exhibited as an artist and even had a show closed down by the police. Yet their place in literary history has been assured through their insertion into the narrative of mainstream modernism, either feeding into it or branching out from it, rather than through postulating a specific avant-garde tradition or even option. This latter course, as we have seen in Acker's case, would mean breaking down the barriers between the history of art and literature, a task for which neither side has been especially enthusiastic or, indeed, prepared. Avant-garde writing has been seen as a necessary phase of experimentalism which, in the carefully chosen words of Malcolm Bradbury and James McFarlane, "made its way by spectacle, establishing its practices and its norms, asserting its distinctive significance for the times," before its achievements were absorbed into a wider current, "the Modernist impulse transcending, often, the tendencies which had pushed and forced forward new modes, new presumptions."

Of course, sexual radicalism was always the third element in this particular story. Stein and Woolf were lesbians and, although they never overstepped the line of literary propriety, even in *Lifting Belly* or *Orlando*, they came very close. Early modernism was intimately entangled with sexual radicalism and the series of scandals and court cases that punctuated its progress were, I would argue, central to its whole project, rather than occasional sideshows. In this respect, too, Kathy Acker's work is in the "great tradition" of literary avant-gardism. In her case, the presentation of sexuality is always bound up with issues of power, violence, and pain, whether explicitly through sadomasochism and rape or implicitly through a generalized oppression. Women, in Acker's books, are both sexually exploited and sexually voracious, an antinomy which generates a cascade of complex discourses, crystallized in the figure of the outlaw heroine, both flaunting her independence, defying her oppressors and bolting in desperation, abject and humiliated. At the same time, the origin of the heroine's sexual confusion and bitterness is always to be found in the nuclear family, in the complex of hollow but unremitting patriarchal authority, resented and yet supported by the desperately submissive mother. The father is a personalized ogre rather than a Lacanian instance of the Law, and the mother is a tragic ruin, rather than a figure of imaginary identification.

After Marcuse—the authoritarian personality and the socialized repression of *eros*—Acker turned to the work of Laing and Cooper, with its emphasis on the repressive dynamics of the family, the entrapment of the child, and the validation of madness as a mode of escape. Acker's adventuresses are always, in some sense, child-women, whose frightening demeanor and impermeable armor vanish to reveal a terrified orphan child, wide-eyed, crumpling up, going "Goo goo," bereft of meaningful words. Then, at the end of the 1970s, she was introduced, belatedly, to the work of Deleuze and Guattari, and found, especially in their *Anti-Oedipus*, a powerful armory of concepts which she could understand as validating, not only the content of her work, but also her rejection of conventional narrative as the reification of desire. Later, she became interested in myth and turned to Sade and Freud as the founding fathers of our primal myths of patriarchy, seen as a machine for generating hysteria and violence. In Acker's work, however, family romance is always inextricably involved with language. Her methodology of writing is worked out within a totalizing discourse in which she speaks from the position of the child, trapped within linguistic double binds and subject to linguistic imperatives which cast her whole identity into doubt. Society is a kind of macro-family of powerful rulers and powerless subjects, terrorizing and terrorized, driving and driven mad—an extreme projection of the psychotic family, and its values, across the whole landscape of interpersonal relations.

In her early writings, the problem facing the heroine and narrator is that of the first-person pronoun, the "I," the linguistic index of identity. Acker appropriated other people's texts, mainly things that had been told to her by friends or, for a brief but crucial period, by fellow workers in go-go dancing joints, and mixed them in with aspects of her own experience, all told in the first person, because, as she put it later, "I didn't want to be like a sociologist." She also changed the genders of her narrator, switching between female and male, between the prison of femininity and the joy of being a pirate. Pirate stories are a constant element throughout her work, childhood fantasies which never lost their charm as she plunged into a world of escape, defiance, and sexual confusion, reinforced by historical research into heroines such as Annie Bonney, the female pirate whose gender was only discovered after her death. As time went on she began to cast herself in a wider, more ambitious variety of roles, as the *poète maudit*, the doomed artist or orphan, the wanderer, the vagrant, the victimized—Toulouse-Lautrec, Pip in *Great Expectations*, Don Quixote (transformed into a dog)—or, more directly, as Cathy from *Wuthering Heights* or Laure, the masochistic lover of Souvarine and Bataille. "I became very interested in the model of schizophrenia. I wanted to explore the use of the word 'I,' that's the only thing I wanted to do. So I placed very direct autobiographical—just diary material, right next to fake diary material. I tried to figure out who I wasn't and I went to texts of murderesses . . . I was doing experiments about memory." Acker's way of writing evolved into a complex mix of Burroughsian cut-ups and "cut-ins," dreams, diary excerpts, foreign-language primers, plagiarism, other people's memories, her own memories, all reduced to the same level of language, told as if by the same narrator, but constantly decomposing the identity of the heroine, changing names, erasing the distinction between the true "I" and the false "I," between the remembered and the invented and the discovered, the text as "found object," the same text repeated in a different context—"the idea that you don't need to have a central identity, that a split identity was a more viable way in the world." In fact, a kind of multiple identity, which could be likened, as Steve Shaviro has suggested, following Klossowski, to demonic possession. Hence, perhaps, the title of Acker's *My Mother: Demonology*, in which she takes on the being of her own dead parent, in a rite of exorcism.

Throughout this process of textual experimentation, Acker stuck fast to her conceptual practices—"I wrote so many pages a day and that was that. I set up guidelines for each piece, such as you'll use autobiographical and fake autobiographical material, or you're not allowed to re-write. I really didn't want any creativity. It was task work, and that's how I thought of it." In another interview she explained that her book, *Kathy Goes to Haiti*, was "mathematically composed: every other chapter is a porn chapter; each chapter, except for the central one, mirrors the facing chapter." Once again, the construction of a text through a predetermined methodology—cut-up or a mathematical procedure or a set of guidelines. As she notoriously confessed, or exaggerated, in conversation with Lotringer, "I don't have any imagination . . . I've used memories, but I've never created stories by making things up." The fantastic elements of her writing are generated textually, rather than by acts of creation—the author is divested of her authority, mediumistic in relationship to a text generated through impersonal methodologies. The narrator, the "I," her/himself, becomes a construct of that text, rather than the other way round. Of course, Acker exaggerated her own absence, but she was speaking from a clear historical and theoretical position—in the background, there lurked Mallarmé's throw of the dice, Roussel's compositional procedures, Oulipo's generated texts, Picasso's *collages*, Duchamp's *objets trouvés*, Rauschenberg's combines, Sade's endlessly rotating tableaux, Olson's distaste for the Romantic ego, Burroughs's cut-ups, Breton's mediumistic ventriloquy, LeWitt's plans and modules, Kosuth's art as idea as idea, Foucault's death of the author.

After she moved to England, in the mid-1980s, Kathy Acker's writing changed again as she turned towards myth as a structuring device—a return to narrative in some ways, but in the form of an impersonal story, belonging to a community rather than to an individual. Acker had studied classical literature as a student— Greek and Latin—and so, once again, she was in a sense, returning to San Diego. Myth had always been there before—voodoo myths especially and then there was her fascination with Bataille—but it took on a new centrality now as a device for structuring the narrative. To Acker, the world of Greek myth was one filled with sexuality and violence, a sense of the marvelous and the inexplicable, of the "Other," with an approach to pain and trauma which she could associate with the rituals of sadomasochism or tattooing—"rites of passage" as she called them, ways of mastering emotional pain through bodily pain, ways of textualizing the body itself. In *Eurydice in the Underworld,* published in 1997, myth becomes a way of exorcizing the fear of death itself. In a theatrical fragment, she cast herself as Electra in a bizarre society drama, set in Sutton Place, her childhood home on New York's affluent and fashionable Upper East Side, and woven around her mother's suicide, which had taken place there twenty years before, yet remained the most emotionally painful event of her life. The author of *My Mother: Demonology* had finally come to terms with the betrayal she felt.

As Acker once put it, "If you scratch hard, you find I'm a humanist in some weird way. Well, humanist, you know what I mean!" In her last books, *Bodies of Work* and *Eurydice in the Underworld,* we find Acker taking issue with Kojève about the end of history, offering her vision of a non-linear narrative time whose chance rhythms offered more than the Hegelian teleology she rejected, agreeing with Hannah Arendt that writers wrote not to express themselves but to communicate with a scattered community of friends, finding more hope in "the meaningfulness of the world" than she had in the past. She was able to abandon the fixated role of traumatized orphan, to die at peace with the worst of her demons. Her voyage was finished at last and she had found the buried treasure. A particular journey was over, but the stories were to go on, the responsibility for reading and writing them carried now by unknown friends, new incarnations of Eurydice and Pip and Janey and the Black Tarantula and all the others. "So the doves cooed softly to each other, whispering of their own events, over Janey's grave in the grey Saba Pacha cemetery in Luxor. Soon many other Janeys were born and these Janeys covered the earth."

Kathy Goes to Hell:
On the Irresolvable Stupidity of Acker's Death

Avital Ronell

Here's my story, sad but true. Georges Bataille has said that we need stories. Kathy Acker adored and devoured Bataille, cannibalizing his language in her last works. Let me back up, then. Yes, I'll begin by backing up, returning to an ostensible starting point, a point of entry.

(The question of friendship brings me to this point. I will be reading the split, especially the split that is figured on many of her book covers—the torn photograph, where she is already figured as the morcellated body. Shortly after she passed away, I began teaching a seminar on friendship and the gift—on the value of non-reciprocity. We were guided by a number of texts and considerations, but especially by recent works of Jacques Derrida. A starting point, offered by Emmanuel Levinas, posits the amorous couple as a figure of injustice, always excluding a third. Bearing this observation in mind, we sought to explore friendship as a crucial modelling of justice. As for me, on the subject of friendship, I have a thing about gathering my friends around me, having them meet or somehow, in a calculable way, cross one another's paths—or pathologies, depending on what configuration of encounter seems more improbable. It's the perv in me, or the hysteric, who likes to stir trouble. Or maybe the desire to hook up friends is more ordinary than all that. It doesn't always have to be science fiction, risking the wrong blend and watching an uncontrollable spill of consequences. Anyway, about two years ago at the airport I introduced Acker to Jacques Derrida. He wasn't greatly familiar with her works, though he knew what she represents for me. I showed him pictures of Kathy and me, one on Kathy's motorcycle.

In it I'm modelling my Japanese look, she's staring sternly at the camera. Derrida liked to get to the airport early, very early. So we normally sat in the Air France terminal and I brought my show and tell. Gil was there, too. I didn't like going home alone after Derrida took off, when it's dark and the world seems dangerous again, unfathomed like childhood. This time I was determined to present some of my thoughts about Kathy's work, to read from some marked passages, to give him a couple of her books for the flight and an early draft of this article, if that's what it is. If you are reading between the lines, and you don't have to be doing so, you can tell that friendship, as I practice it, often involves triangulation and the drama of departure—a straightforward history of flights. Well, straightforward only to a point. I am not always sitting in the airport in anticipation of a heart-thudding separation. Or maybe I am, but it's not always played out so literally, with airport soundtracks and interiors.

Kathy and I sat through all sorts of technological stopovers, we moved through peculiar intersections and shared a highly invested relationship to Europe—mostly, to the more subversive power surges of French and German texts—though, due to a childhood trauma, I was not as big on London as she was, and I haven't yet done Haiti, except to the extent that I "do" anything, namely, through literature and music. To get back to my course on friendship, the first sustained meeting place of Acker and Derrida under my command, I'll sketch the key concerns and trajectories of the arranged rendezvous in what follows. Getting Kathy to go along with me was not so easy. I faced some dilemmas that I should point out at the outset: Kathy Acker and I are not the same; yet, as her friend, I found myself tempted to reduce her to sameness, to love her as a part of me. This reduction implicates me in unjust acts, eliciting as it does a sense of violation: is it possible to remember and engage a friend without the calculation of sameness, without this reserve of narcissistic appropriation? These reflections represent some of the questions that have haunted this piece of writing.

Our title mimes and recites the title of a work for which Acker didn't much care, *Kathy Goes to Haiti*. Nonetheless, I invoke it here because "Kathy Goes . . ." recalls that travelling for Acker was linked to reading. To me, she's still going, still reading.)

1. The Citation

When I first met Acker, it was as if *memory*, mother of the Muses, had been engaged in advance. I had already read her, begun the process of introjection according to a private transferential bureaucracy of self, and remembered her. There was something ass-backwards about our encounter, which occurred as a kind of material extension of a friendship already begun—a constellated relationship already capable of its idiomatic quarrels and turns, complicities and rushes. As in any number of transferential engagements, Kathy preceded herself in my life and already occupied an internal territory of considerable consequence. In a sense, I recognized her at once. To my astonishment, she claimed to know me, too. We found each other immediately—a quirk for which Derrida reprimands Lacanian psychoanalysis, when it claims to find what was always there or meant to be, relying on a kind of metaphysical latency. At the moment of our encounter we said that we had felt destined to each other—in need, in any case, of the comple-mentarity that our writing invited and indicated. We had been writing to one another, in correspondence. Still, she allowed space for the utter strangeness that we each were able to hold; I might have wanted to efface those edges at times but she held steady, keeping her stubborn alterity intact. Today I could say that there was proximity without takeover, invasion with little violation (it would be foolish to deny any trace of violation because Kathy Acker rearranged you on a molecular level, she was that powerful).

For Bataille, friendship is part of the sovereign operation and is linked to reading. It seems necessary and appropriate to begin with a citation from Kathy Acker's corpus. In fact, it would seem to me indecent if I were to refrain from resurrecting a passage from *her* work at this fragile point of entry. In rhetoric citation is called "apostrophe." It is a way of calling to the other and in this place can function as an address to Kathy, from Kathy, to you, through me. As apostrophe, citation opens up as well on what Derrida sees as the possibility of a *post mortem* discourse: it is always the case (no matter what, but especially here) that citation is linked to memory, to acts of bringing back, recalling. When we cite and recite, when we quote the other, we are calling to the irreplaceable one for whom there is no substitute. Acker has written on the subject of memory and in memory of the subject, in *Memorium to Identity*: " 'They teach you stupid things in universities and universities are no good for anybody.' I was angry, though I didn't know why."

There is something about the institution of learning that has angered Acker—something that is associated for her with a studied curriculum of stupidity, the wrong side of memory tracks, heading only for memorization techniques and vital depletion. The site for gathering a certain type of cognitive circumscription, the university was for Acker a destination troubled with the double projectile of desire and repugnance, interest and disdain. She'd send me her CV when she wanted in. She taught at a number of institutions, gladly accepting the invitation of Laurence Rickels to come teach, for instance, at UC-Santa Barbara. At the same time, the university was a dead letter box—not as such bad news for a writer who trafficked in dead letters and parasited the canonic corpus but, still, somehow too numbing, even for her. For all its dumb and numb lethargy, the university issued a menace to her exercise of linguistic promiscuity, threatening at every turn to revoke her poetic license; it put her in a libidinal straitjacket, calmed her roguish stories—wait a minute, I may be mixing us up here and talking about myself. Nothing calmed Kathy Acker, not even the massive institutional tranquilizers which she desired. She remained unsheltered, teaching more or less as an adjunct, bereft of the benefits that would have pulled her out of her medical crisis. I will never get over the fact that Acker had to suffer the refusal of medical benefits. Like many Americans, she was uninsured. No one or no institution should get away with the degradation that was visited upon her, determining her fate. We know that Kathy took out no insurance policies to safeguard thinking or writing, to protect herself against countless intellectual calamities. But that is a wholly other matter . . .

Kathy was aware of the levels of stupor that universities are capable of dispensing; sometimes she needed it and found the stupefying nature of teaching to bring comfort. As far as Kathy was concerned—and she was not alone in this—universities have peculiar transmission problems: they transmit stupidity. Let us retain this hypothesis as we explore the allegorical dimensions of some of these assertions and the predicament in which I find myself as I attempt to scan the resistant complexities of an unreadable friendship.

2. Split Ends

When my contribution to this volume was invited—when Amy Scholder invited me in the first place to speak about Kathy Acker—I was very pleased but I was split. I am tempted to say right now, at this early stage of my reflections on Acker, "end of story": "I was split," story of my life, Amy invited me, I was split; I split—I was simply inclined to bail, to leave. According to the velocities and rules of my own itineraries the "split" has taken me to Heidegger, through his famous *Holzwege* or the multiplication of the fork in roads that lead nowhere. On those paths, and in Kathy's proximity, I learned to differentiate between Heideggerian *Mitsein*—the "being-with" that Jean-Luc Nancy has abundantly explored in his works—and "hanging out." Kathy and I did not so much practice a form of Cartesian-cancelling *Mitsein*. In a sense, without pumping egological energy into our discrete congregation, we simply *hung out* together. We found or practiced a way of accompanying the other without claiming even the minimalist bonds of "being-with." It was something like the complicated structure of "with-without-with" which deconstruction has ventured to explicate. OK, not now. We won't get into it now. Still, I must insist that in my remembrance what needs at times the most attention involves how to read and locate the "with," as in "living with" the other. How does "hanging out," so exclusive to American language usage, displace some of the philosophical traditions of modifying solitude—the *ergo sum*—or creating the encounter, whether it be viewed in terms of a group or polis. In what way was I *with* and also *without* Kathy from the start? What kind of bonds or cuts were inscribed by hanging out with her? (I get anxious. It's been a long time. I miss her. I expect her at any moment to pull me away from the pain of melancholic piety. My first paper on Kathy after her death was in Vermont, at the behest of writer Bob Buckeye. The stumped sense of loss made me freeze.)

If I were Kathy Acker—and in a sense, I am, representing her, I am bringing her here with me, which is why I'm carried by the title, "Kathy Goes to . . ."—if I were she, I would disseminate in the page the way she does in *Blood and Guts in Highschool* with her Persian lexicon, the word "split"—I was split would proliferate ana-grammatically, turning on and against itself, unstoppably splitting with no origin or end, instituting a kind of "spliterature," splitting us up, me and Kathy, though not without memorializing the fact of a singular encounter. We were each in her own right the split subject of which French psychoanalyst Jacques Lacan writes, though our splits were arguably more dramatically transparent than those of the sorry signifiers which he had exposed. We were the sorriest signifiers we had ever known. More on that later.

3. The Trouble with Kathy

But I did not want to begin by risking or invoking the vertiginous splits that characterized the friendship I enjoyed with Kathy Acker. In fact, we were split only on one major issue—it was our *differend*, if I may cite Lyotard's important term, which means a dispute or difference that cannot be resolved by the cognitive or linguistic resources we have at hand. One is simply stranded at a site that offers no legal recourse, knows no appeal, and can't be housed by the rules governing juridical syntax. (In court, it is a matter of what gets through, what's ruled out, such as the suppression of somatic testimony: the blushing, nervous foot shaking, stuttering, tics and "rhetoritics" that make up a legally unassimilable idiom.) It is admittedly a bit grandiose of me to say that Kathy and I had a *differend*—it was at the very least an untouchable pulse of disturbance in the intellectual harmony we shared: she did not approve of my recourse, however critical, to Heidegger, and I did not think that Heidegger was a matter of approval. He (meaning his work) was an event, an irreversible event, not something you could turn your tattooed back on or chose not to read. In any case, Kathy and I were split on the issue of Heidegger, this constituted our *differend*, which neither of us could properly litigate, on which neither of us would budge. I would never have presumed to pull her off Bataille or Rimbaud or some of the other Frenchies she was stuck on. Of course I, too, like my theory with a French accent and in this domain I do not like to split hairs or heirs between the French or Germans . . . But the signifier "split" has carried me off center, I got carried away at the very beginning of a homage to a beloved and irreplaceable friend. I was pushed around by language and got carried off the aim I tried to establish. Language does that to you, pushes you around, I mean, undermining your cognitive grasp of things or the intentional meaning you had hoped to secure. I was not intending to reveal to you that Kathy and I had a disagreement, that we were split on an issue or two. Something from another zone intervened when I wrote that I was pleased to be writing about her but that I was also split about it. I was split for other reasons and according to altogether different registers of anxiety.

It's been a long time since I have turned my thoughts to my lost friend, and she kept appearing, as a site or as a combinatory of barely decipherable letters. This goes to show that you can't secure a mourning target—the object or addressee is susceptible to scandalous substitution, as with love (sometimes, unavowably, you are thinking of someone else and not of the one you're with). Or rather, to be truthful, there were certain people, a number of circumscribed places that started to appear in my dreams. This meant something very powerful was compelling me to return to her. I very rarely am capable of returning to the history of a friendship, as separations are so painful and I imagine only the incessant failures of reappropriations, fearful of the confusing and deluding qualities of returns in general. However, the more I turn away, the more persistently they come at me, the lost friends. Freud predicts this turn of events—he tracks the growing authority of the absent one, the invasive power of the supposedly subdued and classified.

On the other hand, and given another system of splits, I was split because I felt I *must* speak about Kathy Acker. I felt a kind of liability, an obligation; I was pressed by an imperative to honor her. But do these ethical terms, with their inevitably laborious stamp, belong to friendship? Shouldn't friendship be less oppressive, more spontaneous and free, less prescriptive? Yet, it seems I have accepted the assignment, and I do feel that, in a destinal sense (but without being too brusque or creepily appropriative) that Kathy—Kathy, she *was* assigned to me. Still, it was a difficult assignment.

Kathy and I were friends. We spent days and evenings together, years together, in San Francisco and Berkeley, where she and I taught, performed, stirred up trouble, complained, ate, and wrote. We both left the Bay Area at the same time, fed up, tired, narcissistically depleted. We both fell ill at the same time. And according to this logic, I feel we should have both disappeared at the same time. A Deleuzian friend of mine once said, following the Jonestown mass suicides, that there exists a strong desire in us for a synchronicity of death, a wish that we all die at the same moment so that, on the one hand, no one will be left alone, weeping, in a state of inconsolable solitude or, on the other hand, that no one would have to think that the world would go on after her own, very shocking and altogether inexcusable, demise. Ego would like that, if everyone would disappear together: "ashes, ashes, we all fall down." I am not trying to bring you down to my level of torment, however. On the contrary; a poetic sensibility teaches celebration at these moments of radical incomprehensibility. There is something that Derrida says in his book on friendship that I would like to address here as I contemplate the incomprehensible demise of the beautiful and vibrant person and writer that Kathy was. Kathy says in *Blood and Guts* to leave the writer alone; honoring and obeying the sense of her warning to us, I turn my gaze to Derrida, who has anticipated the predicament of the bereaved friend. First, here is what Kathy says, showing up as Hawthorne:

> [I]f you want to publish/help the writer, do it business-like, but don't get into the writer's personal life thinking if you like the books you'll like the writer. A writer's personal life is horrible and lonely. Writers are queer so keep away from them. I live in pain but one day, Hawthorne said, I'm going to be so happy even if I'm not alive anymore . . . Writers create what they do out of their own frightful agony and blood and mushed-up guts and horrible mixed-up insides. The more they are in touch with their insides the better they create. If you like a writer's books read his books, the books aren't pure suffering.[1]

Let this utterance, in which the title is named and situated (the writer's "blood and guts"), take up a place here, and let me return to it with Derrida shortly, when I read Acker and Derrida bifocally. Kathy tells us to keep away from her, to accord her pain some solitude. Though, I must say, doing the job herself, she switches gender and generalizes to mask herself behind a male marked writer, a momentarily masculinized narrator, a universal cipher that dredges her resources, leaving her alone. I am not saying that Kathy was this or that at this point. Her studied inessentialness left her dreadfully alone. She held her poses, even when she offered up the writer's innermost fragility. Kathy's suffering was sheltered by artifice—something that could be said about anybody, except that Kathy, in a sense, coveted her losses. She made a constant play for suffering and dove into the unremitting logic of "asking for it." We cannot simply leave out the possibility that Kathy Acker asked for it.

I would like to speak of bereavement and friendship, of the knowledge of finitude that the friend exposes, but I also do not want to burden the reader with a requiem of sorts, or at least I do not want to hit you with a massive dosage of melancholia, all at once and undiluted. That would be my tendency: all at once, heavy, with a burdened sense of catastrophe. All at once, hit you with it. Everything is a matter of dosage, Nietzsche once said, apropos of history. So let us dose down. (You see, she taught me that: I am a sort of drug dealer, tranquilizing or stimulating according to the highly nuanced writing protocols that she practiced.)

4. On Stupidity: Adorno, Kathy, Henry James

It was a gift, but Kathy had ways of testing your friendship. I am tempted to go over other work now that grew out of our time together. For instance I discussed with her a then work-in-progress, *The Test Drive*, where I trace and explore the figure of testing in our modernity, starting with Nietzsche and what he evaluates as our experimental disposition. I am interested in the limits of testability, the way we are always being tested. The Greeks had a word for it, *basanos*, which links testing to torture. It is not the case that we know when or whether we're being tested (because if you *know* you're being tested, this awareness may collapse the premises of the test—you may consider in light of this cognitive snag the figures of Abraham, Job, Christ or, on another register, Rousseau, who were each submitted to tests of major consequence but without knowing that they were being tested). The modality of the test interested me in light of a chapter I was completing, entitled "Testing Your Friendship." The test of friendship that I explore overtly is organized around the breakup of Nietzsche and Wagner, which Heidegger sees as a historial event, involving the end of metaphysics—involving, in other words, the very way in which we think and make love. This work, like its predecessor, *Stupidity*, grew out of a theoretical concern with testing and about presumptions we make about intelligence and cognitive claims.[2] I discussed my thoughts with Kathy, sketching in her living room the beginnings of these works. I see her sitting in her stuffed chair, listening intently. We had just talked about pirates and leather, a current concern of hers. In her work, "stupid," "stupidity," "idiotic"—words that often accompany Acker's descriptive rants. Sometimes she downshifts to "dumb." There's a difference, however. More biting than asserting that someone is dumb or has done something dumb, which implies innocence or our common existential plight, stupidity by contrast invokes a type of malignancy. So many things are dumb—that you have to go to the bathroom, get a job, get up, go to sleep, watch your weight, check your calls, pay your bills, clean your apartment, get another degree—all this suggests a level of facticity, whereas *stupidity* implicates its object in a certain way, as if malice were intended, as if there were an element of ethical failure involved. In any case, stupidity appears to call for a judgment, if not an outright condemnation. Though it is pervasive and close at hand, stupidity, as theme or topos in philosophy and literature, tends to be left out of the picture, or at least it had remained largely uninterrogated. Attuned to its several registers of usage and intent, Kathy was appalled by stupidity and denounced it wherever it came up, especially in repressive politics or with issues of social justice. Stupidity, such as that of religious fanatics, would put her in a rage. She was in good company. Nietzsche, as my one-time Berlin mentor Jacob Taubes pointed out, collated Christ with a figure of hermeneutic blindness relegated to idiocy. At tea one day I shared with Kathy my findings on the invention of the idiot in philosophy and poetry. I adored Wordsworth's "Idiot Boy," a poem for which he got whacked by his partner in rime, Coleridge. Coleridge, as partner and overseer, wanted Wordsworth to get serious, stay off the path of idiocy, and direct his oeuvre toward the philosophical poem. Then I'd jam on stupidity and by the second glass of wine we'd start talking about how stupid everyone was. It didn't take much. Still, Kathy, being Kathy, was generous in the extreme and could turn values around: on some days, for her, stupidity had a distinctly liberatory resonance.

But what is stupidity, what conditions its contours? Philosophy, with the possible exception of Nietzsche, has generally protected itself from going too far in the direction of stupidity. As signifier, index, a grammatical behavior or impossible object of contemplation, it was something to be dropped, forgotten— even though thinking and cognition themselves depend in the end on some understanding of stupidity. Not even a concept, and barely a paraconcept, it belongs to a kind of theoretical explosion of class warfare: for the most part, philosophy won't deign to address stupidity. In the two pages devoted to the topic in *Dialectic of Enlightenment*, Adorno and Horkheimer view stupidity as a scar, "a tiny calloused area of insensitivity." It is thought to be evocative, moreover, of "the desperation of the lion pacing up and down its cage, or of the neurotic who renews a defensive reaction that has already proved futile in the past."[3]

Literature is more expansive, inclusive, and doesn't mind lowering itself to its most repressed roots. In literature, stupidity occurs as a theme, a genre, a history—but it is by no means identifiable according to secure or established determinations. Henry James's *Washington Square* leaves it undecidable whether Catherine's unbounded loyalty to her lover ought to be viewed as stupid or sublime. Stupidity offers a whirligig of imponderables: as irreducible obstination, tenacity, compactedness, the infissurable, it is at once dense and empty, cracked, the interminable "duh!" of contemporary usage. A total loser, stupidity is also that which rules, reproducing itself in clichés, in innocence and the abundance of world. It is at once unassailable and the object of terrific violence, which is why it drew Kathy's fire—her signifier. On the one hand, the very existence of stupidity can and must be disputed—are we not dealing in each case with intricacies of repression, bungled action, error, blindness?—and on the other hand, stupidity can and must be exposed. In a sense, though, one wonders who would be spared liability where stupidity is concerned. Is there not a suspicion, an anxiety, that you, a fugitive from stupidity, are on the verge of being caught (finally) by some smart bomb heading for your house?

I have been told time and again that Kathy has left her body; she will no longer answer to her name. The adult in me appears to have grasped this unassailable assumption, more or less gesturing toward the stage of grief, which is associated with acceptance. Yet, even today, I try to comprehend why she won't answer my phone calls—I am rendered speechless. That's about all I can say. I am probably prepared only to share the silent part of my grief before the scandal of her death. There was her memorial in New York. Convoked along with other friends, I had brought incense and a Buddhist figurine to the memorial in an effort to please Kathy. They wouldn't let me put the incense inside the art space, on the altar, so I lit it outside and people said you could smell it all the way down the block, near Broome Street, and it functioned like a bell, synaesthetically calling everyone to gather around her absence. I suppose it would be senseless to pursue a memorial of the memorial at this time, conjuring the mood and attestations of her community, although one would like to do so. The memorial had taken place and a community of friends rose to address her in her absence. At the end we applauded long and loudly, with her picture staring back at us. I was broken up.

In so-called life, Kathy Acker created community wherever she went, insistently. Not the Christian or politically suspect kind. Her implementation of community was something she took from Bataille: she insisted on community without relying on transcendence—a community without communion, without fascistic bonding rituals or strangulating close ties. This was a community without illusions about itself but that erupted ecstatically, multiplied addresses, instigated trouble, defied all sorts of instances of social degradation, and in the end didn't even believe in itself or remember its momentary manifestations. Her community was self-annulling. Yet, it remained rigorous. She practiced the installations of community that were unfolded in the singular works of Bataille, Blanchot, and Nancy, who wrote *La Communauté désœuvrée (The Community at Loose Ends)* which thematizes, among other things, a kind of literary communism—something that strongly informs Acker's works. (Nowadays Giorgio Agamben builds on this work and configures community as Kathy would have acknowledged.) The notion of literary communism probably "belongs" to Nancy, if property attribution makes a great deal of sense in this context. In a sense, Kathy shared literature and imparted it freely. Her adherence to an ever fracturing community was reflected in the work to which she appended her name. She practiced literary depropriation, in her exhibitionistic way renouncing property, the proper—any claim to her ownmost inventiveness, "originality"—propriety. It was a point of honor with her, a necessary cut of social transgression. She gave up the mystical foundations of authorship, the capital claims, looting and vandalizing legally protected stores of knowledge. The difference between Kathy and other authors was that she was caught on tape—or, rather, she kept turning herself in to the authorities with that defiant narcissism of a proud troublemaker, a punk criminal. Her bud Burroughs used to say, "steal everything in sight." And she did. Most authors conceal such evidence of a hijacked corpus or they transvaluate theft back into property, with proper holdings, sanctioned attributions and ideologies of "influence." Kathy stole everything in sight and pissed on propriety. I'd show her a text, she'd already be printing it out the next day: her politics of friendship. (In fact, though, she had steered clear of the computer, so this is shorthand for another pirating procedure.) Well, then.

Acker undermined the staple myths of originality, of literary ownership and reliable reference. She rearranged the logic of framing and defied the performative powers of a book's title. The title of a book is a legal institution: it institutes a text and no book can exist without a title. Sometimes Acker would snap up other titles, violently snatching their powers and pilfering histories. Ever dispossessed, she would take from the works of others and claim them momentarily as her own. The effect was to show the dispossession inherent in any text, no matter how familiar, intact, or confidently sealed by a prestigious signature. She ran with the wolves of literary ownership. And yet, she stuck close to home. Kathy Acker scrambled the master codes without pretending that she could simply dispense with them. That's what made her, for some readers, radically effective. She wrote at the borders of a metaphysical tradition, ever negotiating at the limits, without for a second thinking that she could bail. There was no outside or mystified Elsewhere to our literary inheritance. In this sense, Acker was a loyal daughter of a great lineage—she did not turn her back on what was bequeathed to her; to the end, she honored and revered literature: she didn't turn her back on a very determined history of thought or on the literary tradition; she just turned them on their backs, that is, by reinscribing, regendering, profaning, desecrating, shattering the source and adjusting reference in a constant, loyal, determined way.

As for me, I have partially incorporated her voice. I have found myself interiorizing Kathy according to altogether surprising exigencies—it has been surprising to receive her dictations. Like a true neurotic, I have installed sound systems through which Kathy booms words. Though fairly regular, she remains unpredictable: sometimes I am talking to the dean on behalf of my department and the word "cunt" comes up, mid-sentence, in Kathy tonalities ("we're requesting additional funding for a visiting CUNT professor"); and I find myself saying "fucked up" where she might have offered that locution, though I haven't mastered her intonation—my ways of saying such things still line up with Scorsese and Brooklyn, I'm afraid. But what does get said, coming from within me and from beyond me, from Kathy, is "byee!"—her consistent way of saying goodbye.

5. The Good Breast

In any event, and despite it all, Kathy Acker was for me what Melanie Klein pinpoints as the good breast. And like all good breasts, she invites ambivalence and poisoning, a reflex of destruction, as you saw occurring in the first lines of my homage to her. (Freud was vexed when Mrs Klein, as she was called, backdated aggression, making one ready to rocket after just a few weeks of this existence.) Kathy, she was the good breast, nurturing and kind, always giving me things, especially in order to punctuate our meetings. She'd say, as I was leaving, "wait, I want to give you something"—she'd bring out a hat, yes, often a hat (once it was a retro hat with a veil, another time a Harley Davidson knit cap), and other things. As an interlocutor she was very responsive to the most ungeneralizable pathologies of writing; she had precise and refined tastes. I was the beneficiary of her generosity, her light. In terms of acquired inwardness, she taught me about meditation and how to retreat. Sometimes, when you called Kathy, she'd pick up and say, "Honey, I'm meditating, let me call you back."(Later Amy tells me that this habit of hers was hurtful, meaning she didn't consider us important enough to stay on the phone just then. I admit that I was confused by her picking up when she was meditating, but I realized one of its strategic senses only recently when Amy, as said, pointed it out. Maybe Kathy was really meditating a few times when I happened to call, maybe she wasn't trying to get me off the phone each time. Oh-oh.)

About our friendship, of which there is so much residue, so much that still awaits reflection and comprehension, though without comprehensiveness—I shall never catch up with our friendship—about our friendship, there was something old-fashioned *and* inappropriable, new, at the same time. There were literary discussions, support for one another's work. Calls to say we had read something that the other had published, we were blown away, we were thinking about x, y or z that had been asserted. This seemed to me old fashioned; we could have been eighteenth-century correspondents, corresponding to one another, responding, responsible. She energized what the German poets of that era called *Ge-spräch*, emphasizing the "co" in correspond or, more literally, in conversation. In this sense, she was reliable, to be counted on. But she was also rigorously perverse in a way that I found exhilarating, getting us thrown out of restaurants on Sunday afternoons, pissing off people, uncompromising, punching a hole in any man-ifestation of family values. This woman, Kathy, practiced zero tolerance for the insolence of valuations derived from family, religion, or state. The load of crap she had to fend off, even from well-meaning lefties, sometimes strained her more private hegemonies. She was always getting in a fight with someone.

It has been hard on me, responding to a nearly prescriptive invitation, to write on or for Kathy Acker. What struck me as particularly difficult was the necessity of including myself in a narrative. The requirement of constructing such a narrative filled me with dread, as if I were attracting bad luck. Who am I to eulogize Kathy Acker—and then, how could I not, is it not a duty, a responsibility of friendship? I was double-bound to her by the rules of friendship and the law of finitude. In much of my work I had concerned myself with the duties of the survivor, be it Johannes Peter Eckermann, who took dictation from Goethe even after the great poet's death, or Alexander Graham Bell, who connected up with his departed brother, fatefully heading for the electrician, Watson's, bench. Yet, when, philo-sophically speaking, is one *not* paying duties or energetic taxes to the departing other? Is there any discernible duty-free zone in friendship? (There ought to be—but "ought" belongs to prescriptive registers, is duty-bound.) The friend leaves you . . . with a number of pressing questions, a number of pressure points susceptible to unceasing pain. When did Kathy start leaving me? Did she have leave to take leave? Permission and leave permeated our sustained encounter. It is hard to stop thinking about when it started ending between us.

. . . And has this rapport to her essential finitude begun only after her death, or does not every friendship figure the death, the mortality of the friend? Isn't friendship somehow based on this knowledge—the prescient knowledge that you must go, that one of us must go? Again, these questions have nettled Derrida's thinking ever since we asked him long ago in Berkeley, pressing him with naïve intensity, what he thought about friendship. You asked Derrida a question or showed him a postcard and a book sprung up; you told him you were a vegetarian and he produced the thought of carnologocentrism. Jacques was like that—Kathy, according to her own algorithms of absorbing the other, too.

I return incessantly to the bereavement implicit in the very possibility of friendship. The terms for offering love are welded to an experience of mourning, particularly if one follows Aristotle's roadmap for adoring the great friend. One is exhorted by Aristotle to love the other as one would love the deceased. Loving your friend tenderly is modelled on the way you might love your ancestors, a departed lover, the absentee poet—whether or not they will answer to your loving, whether or not there could be reciprocity or some promise of specularity, of loving you back. True love of friendship has relinquished any economy of return or requital. I have to interrupt myself here and confess my uneasiness as I write: in the first place, so unaccustomed to saying "I" in my texts, so comfortable in the practice, nearly Zen, of the attenuation of the subject, the effacement of self and the radical passivity exacted by writing—it is very shocking to me to have to include myself in this unnuanced way. I could handle myself as a barely audible trace in the service of some alterity to be addressed, but saying, for me, brazenly, "I" makes me shudder. Especially when it comes to Kathy. "I" is vulgar, or so goes my prejudice and practice. But this is a problem due to friendship itself.

6. Who Is She?

Split between two poles that do not form a polarity, I am caught. Reflecting on Kathy Acker, on assignment, makes me examine the disjunction between *narcissism* (where I claim the friend is a part of me) and *alterity* (I cannot appropriate the friend to myself or exercise a narcissistic reappropriation of sorts, operate a reduction of the friend to the same or to the friend as other). The paradoxes and aporias posed by this disjunctive crevice are manifold. Sometimes I am seduced by the possibility of giving in to proximity—I have pulled Kathy in, close to me, and I want to accomplish the fusion of you and me. But then I remember Nietzsche's lessons, the call to maintain or keep a relentless distance within a good friendship. To keep it separate, as we did for the most part in life. What Nietzsche emphasizes—this becomes important for Bataille but also for a liberationist politics—is a domestic policy of *disidentification*, the necessity of separation in order to make friendship and something like community possible. Hence the non-Christian communion, the pulling apart that he sees in terms of an infinite wrenching. (In another idiom, on a decidedly rhetorical register, this energized separateness could be read as belonging to the frugal gains of irony and allegory: yielding a politics of allegory, that is, of noncoincidence, it institutes a covenant of the severed.) The Nietzschean severance policy is opposable to political tendencies toward unification that assert a mystified oneness, as in Heidegger's usage of the terms "gathering," "*das Heilige*" (holiness, a problem for Levinas, to which he opposes *sainteté*) or *Volk*. Nietzsche versus Heidegger, but that's another story. (Kathy and I shared many Germanic tropes, philosophemes, and itineraries. We especially shared Nietzsche.) Nietzsche argues for the necessity of the dissociated, singularized, *vereinsamt* (isolated, alone), for that which is constituted by monadic alterities. So he asserts the necessity of resisting what I have been calling the fascistic fusion, the oneness that characterizes key phantasms of totalitarianism and attempts at totalization. As indicated, the exorbitance of individuation goes against the grain of the Heideggerian gathering, grinding down the instances of gathering in which the *Volk* congeals into a politics of one and sameness. Instead, we have *laceration*, the cuts and break-off points that punctuate communication— much of which is handled in Nancy's reading of Bataille, where he draws up a plan for an untethered community, shifting the grounds of the desired erasure of difference. A nonsubstantial domestic policy, laceration offers a political *Liebestod* averted. No one gets mashed up in the political machine as a work, as a substantial project that swallows you whole.

Good friendship, then, for Nietzsche requires that we affirm the break and enact the split-off points.[4] Friendship, if it is to be marked up as "good" in the noble Nietzschean sense, is not the narcisstic glom-on, though God knows he practiced it with Wagner: "Ich bin Du, Du bist Ich," as Tristan and Isolde say to one another, one as other or rather, one and the same. "Good friendship" supposes disproportion. One considers the modulations of friendship that bound Schleiermacher to Schlegel. Schleiermacher defended his best friend from theory-bashing but privately confided to him that he understood very little of what his friend was up to. I love you to death but, honestly, I can't make sense of your writing. Schlegel responds that nonunderstanding guarantees friendship, makes it a permanent translating practice and tender holding pattern. It is imperative that good friendship be unbound from the yoke of understanding—who would be so deluded as to claim to understand the friend? Who would demean the beloved friend by finding her transparent or readily intelligible? Good friendship demands a strong measure of rupture in reciprocity or equality, as well as the interruption of all fusion or confusion between you and me. Born of disproportion, it is evidenced, claims Nietzsche, when you respect the other more than yourself. This cast of friendship commands that one abstain prudently from all confusion; wisdom asks that one surrender the wish-fulfillment of merger between the singularities of you and me. Why dwell on Nietzsche's concept of a good friendship? The good friendship, borne of disidentification, enables you to *see* your friend. When you identify with your friend, you don't see her, you are blinded by him; empathy has replaced understanding. Understanding, on the other hand, presupposes differences and distance, pivoting on the Nietzschean tact of *Dis-tanz*. When distance is bridged you cannot see each other; instead, you are thrown off by this narcissistic extension that the other, as appropriated by your identification, has become.

Essentially a gift, friendship dissolves the economy of give and take yet retains an ethical strain. Friendship at once obligates you but also absolves you of all obligations. A friendship made or kept out of duty would not qualify as a good friendship. Thus the logic of the gift elaborated in Derrida's several works on the topic reorients our more common understanding of friendship, calling it back to the aneconomic terms of nonreciprocity, dissymmetry, or disproportion.[5] The political consequences of such a rupture in reciprocity, particularly in regard to democratic formations, are considerable. Nietzsche puts us on a search for a justice that would break with sheer equivalence—something that Levinas explores in altogether different tonalities and philosophical circumstances. What would be a concept of equality, an equity, which would no longer be calculated according to our systems of equivalence? Or a political structure that would inscribe a movement beyond proportion or appropriation, exceeding thereby all love of the proper? Traditionally, friendship has modelled politics, which is why they are often anamorphic of one another, mirroring and distorting, calling the other to order, working without respite on justice and the possibility of being a good friend—perhaps offering a little more in the life of political tryouts than the merely "good-enough" relative, with which familial formations must be satisfied. If justice cannot be served in the precincts of friendship, why bother magnifying the scope to more politically assigned domains? But the politics of friendship involves all sorts of recesses and temporal complications, implicating structures and para-concepts from which an overhaul of political theories may benefit. The friend, in one sense, has not yet arrived, even after her departure. Perhaps the same can be said for democracy or the historical experience of justice.

Wherever she is, ahead of me or behind me, I expect the friend; I am pregnant with her. I carry her for an interminable term. How do I comprehend my condition or my conditionality in terms of the friend? How is it that I still carry him to term? Derrida has asserted that there is no friendship without philosophy, and no *philosophia* without *philia*: these terms are indissociable. Which is why, when it comes to friendship, one reflects and thinks—one reads and loves and thinks, together or apart. (Thinking, Heidegger often suggested, indicates a kind of piety; it is related to thanking.) Thinking and thanking are inextricably linked: I thank you means I think you. To the extent that I thank (think) you, I am called by you. The call comes from within me and beyond me.

Who needs friendship? Well, in a sense, being and time require it. You are timed by your capacity to befriend. There is an exquisite temporal dimension to devoted friendship. To love friendship is to love the future. This is how Nietzsche figures it; for him, the friend *is* the future. The friend promises the future, which means that she splits the performative qualities of the promise by holding down the fort in a present that, in order to assert itself, already inhabits the future. A different temporality appears to govern Derrida's reading of friendship, though his thought maintains, in any case, a futural inflection. Friendship, according to Derrida, opens up the experience of time. The apprehension of survival constellates time and a relation to lived life as that which already exceeds the living; hence, the languages that underscore sur-vival (*sur-vie, über-leben*). Derrida locates in surviving the origin and essence of friendship. Not empirical or chronologically clocked but funda-mental, the structure of surviving means that one of you will be left behind, responsible and responsive to the intemporal, and largely irretrievably mute other. The itinerary can get complicated, as in the case of Eckermann, who played dead after Goethe's departure and let the poet dictate to him in the long night of their refused separation. Or, again, there was the cable that Aleck Bell threw to his dead brother, beginning a massive history of telecommunications which, no matter how currently dispiritualized, continues to offer the promise of reaching out and touching the absent other. Disavowed and forgotten, there is a survival guide coiled into every phone call, every attempted connection.[6] These slightly aberrant structures and histories themselves respond to a call more prior and essential. There is something about loving the friend that is, from the start, pitched on the grieved act of loving, which is to say, when you become friends, when you fall for the friend, you already acknowledge the finitude that defines the friend. The anguished apprehension of mourning haunts and plunges you, the loving friend, before mourning, into mourning.

The experience of friendship involves the eventful matter of the other's withdrawal. This is why friendship oriented toward the deceased establishes for Derrida a basic structure of friendship as such. In English we say that friends are "made," implying a creative effort or, at the very least, a performative constitution of friendship. When you make friends, you dwell in the light of a bestowal: the making of friends implies that a gift has been granted, or enabled, a space has been opened for a kind of exorbitant giving. Yet, because *poiesis* or making is involved, this space is torsed by the oscillating moments of labor and gift in which it is construed. Friendship is held together, we could state in a Kantian mood, as purposiveness without purpose. The trace of making the friendship, making it *work*, remains in the working, as a work—even when it doesn't work. The subtle tension between work and gift appears to recede yet does not let itself be forgotten. Vital reflections on friendship rarely point to the work force that keeps the amity going, not even in the historial suffering, as Heidegger intimated, that set Nietzsche apart from Wagner in the end. Nietzsche, for his part and partition *made* the break-up, affirming its necessity as a way of reading the friendship. The break is already there, from the upbeat, which is why Wagner discredited or Wagner beloved belong to the same reading program at the end of philosophy. Nietzsche was moving in on the absent recipient; he switched soundtracks on Wagner, but for very determined reasons.[7] So, then: exemplary friendship embraces, in a resolutely unrequited way, an unwearied capacity for loving generously without being loved back. Marking the limit of possibility—the friend need not be there—this structure recapitulates in fact the Aristotelian values according to which acts and states of *loving* the other are preferred to the condition of *being-loved*, which depends for its vigor on a mere potentiality. Being loved by your friends just pins you to passivity. For Aristotle, loving, on the contrary, constitutes an act. To the extent that loving is moved by a kind of disclosive energy, it puts itself out there, shows up for the other, even where the other proves to be a rigorous no-show. Among other things, loving has to be declared and known, and thus involves an element of risk for the one who loves and who, abandoning any guarantee of reciprocity, braves the consequences when naming that love.

7. The End, My Only Friend, the End

Every encounter with the friend has also borne this attestation: I do not survive the friend; in fact, the friend who encounters me in my mortality, already bears my death, which is thus expropriated in advance. Such an attestation appears to go against the grain of Heideggerian claims made on behalf of the absolute aloneness of one's death, which, in its infiltratable ownness, no other *Dasein* can take up for you. Heidegger's essential insight cannot be refuted. Yet even he, in *Being and Time*, had installed the ghostly voice of a friend in such a way as to mortally shake up the absolute aloneness of which he wrote. Friendship enacts a scene, however displaced or repressed, of the friend's disappearance—or, through the friend, it scores a secret knowledge of one's own demise. Friendship maintains a holding pattern over the separating distance, taking place, in the first—and last—place, without attestable proximity. Such is the lesson handed down to us from the Aristotelian model of loving the dead, loving without reciprocity, to Nietzsche's assertion of disproportion and distance in friendship. Reading the transmissions filtered through Aristotle and distributed by Nietzsche, Derrida installs the temporal qualities of survival that inform the possibility of friendship from the start. There have been different ways to state these experiences of friendship and the quasi-betrayals built into the very structure of loving the friend. For Nietzsche, friendship unfolds without the bolstering guarantors of proximity or presence but is kept among a population of solitudes; favorable intimacy abides in an ensemble, or perhaps, rather, among a spectrology of those who love in separation, at a distance and in withdrawal.

Acker dedicates a section of her book, *My Mother: Demonology, a novel* "(to B, who's dead)." She limits her inscription to the letter "B," but we can hear it homonymically as a cipher for Being, as stating "to be or not to be, who's in any case dead." The section is titled "My Dream Showed Me That I Don't Belong Among Respectable People."[8] Kathy, writing to the dead, dedicating to the dead, making friends, conversing with the departed. In another section, she avows her loyalty to reading, a figure, for her, of true amity—but not in order to become intelligent, she warns:

> "Right after I saw him, I wrote . . . in my secret notebook . . . I'll travel and travel by reading. I won't read in order to become more intelligent . . . I knew from the first moment I was that I hated them, the hypocrites." As soon as I had written this down I knew that I was dreadfully and magnificently alone.[9]

8. Ugh!

Another way to have approached Kathy would have been to delineate her theory of prophecy. Much of what Kathy had to say was prophetic, hence her particular brand of irony. In the same novel, she opens a section called "Dreaming Politics" with these questions: "Where does Bush's power stop? Where does an authoritarian leader's power stop? Tell me, Mommy, where and how will Bush's power stop?"[10] She saw the terrifying lineage, the future history of spilt blood.

. . . Oh, the history of blood. I forgot to say that the book cover is bright red. Yes, red. Here's another red thread that I would have wanted to follow (I cannot stop reading Kathy, finding it impossible to let go, to end). The narrator states that she loves the color red. Her unconscious turns up in red. Under the opening section, "Into That Belly of Hell Whose Name is the United States," she opens the novel with the subtitle "My Mother": "I'm in love with red. I dream in red."[11] Further along, she affirms that "red gave me the authority to be other than red . . . In me dead blood blushed crimson into the insides of roses and became a living color that's unnameable."[12] OK, I finally know how I should have begun to write about Kathy. Now that I have reflected on her romanced red, it becomes clearer to me. To do some justice to Kathy's thought, I should have begun with the utterance, signalled under a somewhat representational drawing, "my cunt red ugh." It's so obvious to me now. This is where she locates the matricial origin. Now, when it has become too late, I understand where my friend and mistress would have wanted me to start, where I might have begun on the path of a worthy homage. Oh, Kathy! It's all in this endless little phrase. The repugnance and desire, the unreadable "ugh" that blossoms forth from the red cunt, that which we presume to have read. You wanted me to begin by reading the red "ugh," at once asignificatory and polysemic, but in the first place barely linguistic: a heave, a groan, a punctuation, a way of marking your beautiful, unmystifiable cunt. Ugh! Now it dawns on me, the way you pull away from your own boldness, you avert your gaze with a grunt—is it guttural or soft, maybe hoarse? I am trying to hear you—in this nearly visceral moment, your sigh and your sign, the way you pull away, the distress held in an autocritical sputter. Ugh. I think of Alkmene's famous last words in Kleist's drama: "Ach!" The great drama *Amphitryon* ends unreadably on "Ach"—almost your name, Acker, *Acher*. Ugh. Your unbearable red cunt: how you were and weren't re(a)d.

Notes

1. *Blood and Guts in High School: A Novel* (New York, Grove Press, 1989), p. 100.
2. *Stupidity* (Urbana and Chicago, University of Illinois Press, 2002).
3. Max Horkheimer and Theodor W. Adorno, "The Genesis of Stupidity," in *Dialectic of Enlightenment*, trans. John Cumming (New York, Continuum, 1986), pp. 157, 257.
4. More about breaking up and Nietzschean modalities of self-testing in *The Test Drive* (Urbana and Illinois, University of Illinois Press, 2004).
5. See Derrida's discussion of Nietzsche and friendship in *Politics of Friendship*, trans. George Collins (London and New York, Verso, 1997).
6. The umbilicus of the forgotten phone call—what Nietzsche calls the telephone to the beyond—is one of the traces I put on the genealogy of technology in *The Telephone Book: Schizophrenia, Technology, Electric Speech* (Lincoln and London, University of Nebraska Press, 1989).

7. I discuss Nietzsche's break-up with Wagner, which bore grave consequences for metaphysics, more fully and perversely in "Testing Your Friendship: Or, Breaking Up,' in *The Test Drive*.

8. *My Mother: Demonology, a novel* (New York, Pantheon Books, 1993), p.153.

9. Ibid., p. 17.

10. Ibid., p.174.

11. Ibid., p.7.

12. Ibid., 14.

Acker Un-Formed

Carla Harryman

1. Forward for to with Acker/Child/Wonder-Wander/Labyrinth

My experimental prose work, *Property* (1982), begins with these lines:

> "Come you are a mad revolutionary," said her uncle with a smile. He pointed at the wildflowers. "My vision of the aspects I more or less fortunately rendered was exactly my knowledge."[1]

In this instance the figure for revolution is revolutionary because, in the uncle, vision and knowledge meet. His elocutionary gestures strapped to solipsistic, airtight content point toward meaning that is non-transferable, and for "the niece" impossible. Her revolt is based on negation. This same figure, the niece, when her auntie quotes Socrates thusly, "When one thing is entirely different from another, it cannot be in any respect capable of behaving like the other, can it?" . . . protests, "Auntie, Auntie, this child is not yet formed." The child, who is not really a child, but a figure for she who is subordinated within various communal, discursive, and lived contexts, is in a double bind: her revolt is to reject the relations to language that make her an outcast: she wants knowledge but the codes of knowledge are inadequate. The radical redistribution of language conventions in *Property* is the imaginary reformulation of the terms of discourse/language as property; it is an example, a language-along-the-way, that can indicate a place where the child/infantilized/subordinated subject has agency.

The problem with this narrative of *Property* is that the characters become in my description here focal points when in fact they are as if figures of speech; the figure/word/object is presented in bits and pieces throughout the collaged fantasy-inflated prose and is a "property" itself of prose, a property that has been deregulated and redistributed. There are similar problems in discussing the personae, the narrative, and the prose spaces of Acker's novels.

2. "Multieverything:"[2] Space and Spacing

One can think of the emblematic figures in Acker's later fictions as anarchic functions that don't take root as fictional subjects but that instead possess unreliable properties that crowd the space of the novel such that they *don't* come to represent effects of pirated texts or fictional subjectivities. Neither do they exactly *lack* character/subjectivity—rather it seems that they are in an altogether different circumstance: one in which subjectivity, the illusory hallmark of character, is not a concern. These Ackerian figures occupy a space/world that is all over—as in ubiquitous—and their anarchic operations are productive of the impossible all-over spaces of the book.

Thivai, a principal figure in *Empire of the Senseless*, is, for instance, at different and all points a vessel through which the novel in *Empire* pours Abhor's biography, a bi-gendered monster, a hooligan or Tom Sawyer's replacement, the name of modern-day Thebes, a figure that performs the same function as a character in *Neuromancer*, the narratological voice of William Burroughs—and well one could go on, which is one of the traps Acker's novels lay for anyone who tries to write about them. The reader of an Acker work suspends her own interpretive coherence; self-identity in reading multiplies, expands, pixelates, contracts, is undone: the reader becomes to herself a multisensory/sensibility of the text, a further anarchic layer of the text and/or obstruction. Reading further crowds the text. "I" am interference.

The conflation/diffusion of character/reader within text anarchy reminds me of Denis Hollier's use of the term "a-subjectivity" in his book *Against Architecture: The Writings of Georges Bataille*. A-subjectivity is a product of the space of the writing, "that would not allow for the time to become a subject."[3] Acker's writing is architectonically both planar (slippy-slidy) and networked (branchy). The philosophical space of the novel is transcendent, simulacral, and unravelling-from-the body all in the same space. The diversity and complexities of aesthetic and intellectual spaces in Acker's work, I think, contribute to the effects of a-subjectivity Hollier discusses in Bataille's work.

For this volume, I am interested in associating the difficult spaces of the writing with a kind of unformed subject, the subject "wonder" (a word Acker uses in her later work) compels. The I/eye "comes upon" language, and this is what Acker claims she is "only interested in" by 1995 in her essay "Seeing Gender."[4] Acker associates wonder with several other words including "myth" and "labyrinth." However, these words, like everything else about her writing, are not neatly nested one into the other. Even if it doesn't account for the total space of the novel, the Ackerian labyrinth[5] is mind-bogglingly multiple in its meanings, values, and functions. Here are some of the ways I think about Acker's labyrinth: it is a pre-existing referential structure, a mythic artifice in the making, the sign of an anti-monumental, distributed rather than hierarchic architecture, complexity itself, the place where the Minotaur was slain or not slain, a narrative site in which Acker intervenes with contradictory revisions of the myth of the Minotaur, a material extension of the body analogous to language, a product of "seeing" and/or the imagined site of writing as meditation and desire. In Acker, pre-existing structure and the unknown are often conflated and or collapsed one into the other, and this produces more complexity, more labyrinth within the space of the novel. Labyrinth is also the logical and spatial site of myth, but myth is as unstable in her writing as structure.

3. The Not-Yet Labyrinth Passage to the Open Dream

The original title of this essay, "This Is a Living World"[6] or "Against Ordinary Language"[7] was composed from Acker's own words, and was meant to point to Acker's use and consideration of language as connectedness, a language that is and makes reality. Along the way to this essay, I became interested in the architecture, or anti-architecture, through Hollier's reading of Bataille, of Acker's later novels and found myself wandering in a slightly more complex and also unformed space for reading Acker's work and notebooks, especially as I came to associate the condition of wonder with regression in general, regressive diction in particular, and the ventriloquy of childhood.

A developmental narrative about her oeuvre can be located in Acker's interview with Sylvère Lotringer[8] and in her essays and her commentary on her writing. This narrative describes a progression from autobiographical to conceptual art literature, through nihilism and deconstruction, to a writing of discovery through myth.

Acker associates the myth-making desire and drive with the labyrinth and wonder. The fabrication of a mobile and unstable labyrinthine structure as novel-writing and as disclosure of (sub)consciousness is what potentially produces connectedness, and a writing of multieverything.

The active disclosure of Acker's writing in her later novels is paired to another more open and passive kind of disclosure, one that entails intense and almost predatory curiosity: a reader of Acker's later works (and a few of her earlier works such as her creative essay "Realism for the Cause of Future Revolution") would be aware of a marked anterior scanning of the writer's I/eye receptively tracking, like a little fox silently following a juicy chipmunk, textual revelation.

What is missing within Acker's simple publicity narrative about her writing's development, for example the story that takes us from autobiography to conceptual art to deconstruction and nihilism to myth, is that her practice is additive not subtractive. She doesn't leave anything behind. Acker's language of labyrinth (theoretical/construction) and revelation (openness/experience) is an ongoing desiring system, the goal of which becomes to contact reality as revelation of the unknown. The overlays of edifice and openness are related in her later works to childhood as both an institution and as unformed states of being that allow the text/world to be revealed and learned rather than already known.

Acker's chapter "Redoing Childhood: The Beginning of the History of Dreams," in *My Mother: Demonology* narrates two kinds of education. The first is corrupt and institutional:

> The second and only other acceptable method by which we could leave school was to extend our education. . . . My parents and teachers, aware that I will not by nature marry a rich man, explained to me that by attending a top college I still kept the possibility of a "rich" or "decent" marriage.
>
> Refusing all these alternatives, I left school for a world without language in which I had no language . . .[9]

When Laure, our narrator, a French diarist, Bataille's mistress, Acker, etc., sorts out the problem of elitism and education, she enters wonder via the anteroom of education, dancing school, or her own body, where she becomes sexually aroused for the first time. This second kind of education is amoral rather than corrupt:

> And so I learned that any boy, if he does it in my ear, will do.
>
> It is this amoral world, the one of constant wonder, journeying sights that amaze, in which I received and continue to receive my real education. Even if, now that I'm an adult, that world no longer bears only the name *sex*.
>
> The beautiful world that lies outside the school to which they sent me! Sometimes the setting sun is a series of liquid fires that illumine the deer clustered together on the hillsides.[10]

When the edifice of institutionality dissolves, wonder occurs. And it is as if the language matter of the novel spills down upon the edifice of the novel, shifting its levels, obscuring, obliterating, revealing it, and reflecting it/"its face before the creation of the world" as if the novel were the frontal features of a consciousness that precedes the fixity of mind–body splitting.

Thus the world/novel like the child or adolescent is "un-formed." In this unformed world one considers the collapse of myth into the circumstance that precedes it. One imagines the child/animal (Minotaur/monster) is not yet slain, or that Echo has not yet been cast into the forest, or that categorical knowledge is not yet fixed, and trauma can contact the mentality that precedes it. This is a world/novel anterior to a rigid, clogged, dead reality.

4. The A-Subjective Passage in which We Meet Echo

In her essay, "Echo, Irony, and the Political," Denise Riley refers to the figure of Echo as she who "explodes categories from within." The "multieverything" new-narrative effects springing from the myth quests of Acker's later work can in part, I think, be associated with the dubious powers that Riley has assigned to the figure of Echo in her essay. For Echo, as Riley states, occupies language where "the word has the inbuilt capacity to interrogate itself, a latent capacity sparked into life by the truncated repetition which is both Echo's doom and forte."[11] Acker's novel-labyrinth is in part built on last words the words of pre-existing texts whose narratives, characters, syntax, styles are repeated in truncated form. Her style *is* an interrogation of the language.

The life-spark of repetition and truncation in Acker is abrasive, parodic, funny. By appropriating potentially everything, Acker as Echo can keep the echo going indefinitely: the sources for interrogation are virtually inexhaustible. Therefore Acker's/Echo's language as tragic signal or sign of trauma, through its inexhaustibility, approximates or imitates Acker's/Echo's comedic situation before she/it/we/thing/they were cast into the forest of already formulated mythic narrative/novel-writing before fiction had to resemble a novel to be narrative writing. And before subject and object were categories.

What precedes Echo's vocal imprisonment and language atrophy is her excessive talkativeness. I would compare this notion of excessive talkativeness to Acker's obsessive retelling of family dramas and/or her obsession with school in *My Mother: Demonology* in which she appears to make an account biographical, autobiographical, and fictional of every recoverable instance of her/Laure's education. I'll leave it to say here simply that this revisiting of subject matter involves a pleasure the reader can associate with a kind of talkativeness that serves as a bridge to pre-traumatic feelings. It is the imagined or contacted pre-traumatic feeling that in Acker's later fiction produces a world whose effects come before "time, order, and logic." The fantasy of pre-traumatic disorder is made adjacent to or added to the nihilism/deconstruction of her earlier books.

5. Against Architecture or the Turn in the Labyrinth that Brings Us to Hollier

"Great monuments rise up like levees, opposing the logic of majesty and authority to any confusion," writes Denis Hollier in the introduction to his tome on Georges Bataille, *Against Architecture.*[12]

Confusion is a word to regard with something like respect. In the realm of Acker's confusionism, human and rat are conflated. Typical ideological couplings, for instance the male and female of the species, or the reproductive institution of the novel, are violated, often with comic violence ("The male half of me will rape the female half of me, which I know, isn't very nice, but what can you do in a society which doesn't recognize human needs . . ."). The stable effects of narrative logic rest on what Hollier might identify as unstable "unedifying" or "amoral/unearned" narrative architecture. An example in *Empire of the Senseless* involves the narrative of Thivai's imprisonment and escape, except that there is no narrative other than a sensation of narrative as there are no events or even language games (which sometimes instigate actions, e.g. "an act of will kept the fiction of 'me' going") that *cause* his escape; he just walks out. When Thivai walks out, the jail becomes one-dimensional. It is no longer inside the representation of institutional practices and thus Thivai is *not a subject* of these practices.[13]

Acker produces *something* like the anti-architecture Hollier ascribes to Bataille's project, a *something* that "open[s] up a space anterior to the division between madness and reason" in Bataille and also between nonsense and sense or child and adult in Acker; rather than performing the subject, it performs spacing: a space from before the subject, from before meaning; "the asubjective asemantic space" that Hollier identifies as an "unedifying architecture, an architecture that would not allow space for the time needed to become a subject."[14]

6. The Further Passage de Confusionism: Regression-Language Games and Language in the Pre-Politics of Childhood

In Acker, the a-architectural narrative space of the novel is frequently collapsed into the yet-to-be-formed mentality of the child. Childhood is the site of trauma and the pre-traumatic dream and the site of regression in the novel. The youthful utopian "wishful" thinking ventriloquized by Abhor/Huck at the end of *Empire* is expressed in an intensified regressive diction. Abhor the part-robot/Huck sounds not like Twain's Huck but a five- or six-year-old when in this regressive mode:

An then I thought that, one day, maybe, there'ld be a human society in a world which is beautiful, a society which wasn't just disgust.[15]

In *Pussy King of the Pirates*, gender is marked by "girl" and "boy." Adults don't exist and nested stories have been popped out of their nests. Stories are "recited" in the manner of a child telling about what happened and making something up in an all-mixed-up fashion.

The Last Story that I Read

The girl who looked like me and the boy had been living together for years and years. Though they weren't any older.

She wanted to have a baby. He didn't want to, and he didn't want her to, either.

The girl was looking at her body, which had become a graveyard because the boy wouldn't help her make a baby grow in it. She didn't ever want to fuck anyone else.

Inside this graveyard, skulls sat on top of brown dirt replete with holes; here and there, an animal leg; ducks swam on top of green and dead pools.

She looked down, below the graveyard, where she saw a rat. It was a baby. Five strands of hair, all that it possessed, sprouted out of its head. It sat itself right on her lap.

"But I can't have a baby," said the girl.

It held up its front paws, drew her face into its. Its lips, softer than it was possible for flesh to be, wanted to drink her, for she was a pool of water to the baby.

She bent down to her child, who also was crying, and lifted it up. Kissed, suckled it until all loneliness was gone.[16]

Power of choice, power to do adult things, to give birth, to destroy things, to chatter about death and love without repression, and to find love outside the family are part of the dialogues and narratives that children make up when they play house and play with dolls. High and low language is mixed while logical syntax is deployed at the service of make believe. Refined diction along with words and phrases learned from fairy tales and movies are mixed with unsophisticated strings of phrases. This is the language of the child's mingled knowledge and wishes:

After she had stopped being hurt, the girl was able to make distinctions. She perceived that the rat was her lover.

So she laughed and said, "Boys are rats." Then, she and the boy held hands and were happy.[17]

In her essay "Realism for the Cause of Future Revolution," Acker tells us, "I see what I see immediately; I don't rethink it. My seeing is as rough or unformed as what I'm seeing. This is *realism*: the unification of my perceiving and what I perceive or a making of a mirror relation between my world and the world of the painting."

Here is an example of that mirror:

Maybe he wants food. Maybe this is why the female skull's eyes're popping out of her skull: she's happy because she has the bowl of soup. She's not eating it: she doesn't need to eat it. Her spoon is pointing toward the bowl because she owns the food. Ownership is enough. The male skull is lower and deader than her. Ownership, for old people, is everything.

There are no children in this world.[18]

Here Acker imitates a child's view of the painting. Through the de-sublimated imagination of the child, she instructs on two things: one that ownership is everything and two that there are no children in this world. The child's language is a language of contact, and the connection exists in an anterior spacing where "there is no room to be a subject." The trauma is registered by the fiction of Acker as child savant outside the painting and by the absence of the child in the world of the painting.

At this moment in Acker's childlike depiction or anti-architectural reading, there is no discussion of composition, or paint, or manner of painting, there is no citing of date or historical contact; there is story. Story as regression is an instrument of the childtrope. The child is the figure of subordination and erasure, and Acker's regressive storytelling deviously accesses the ignorance of the mentality that lives in the monumental economies and ideologies of a Western culture that displaces rough/difficult knowledge with "educated" observations about surfaces.

Notes

1. Carla Harryman, *Property* (Berkeley, CA., *Tuumba*, 1982), np.
2. Kathy Acker. See "Colette," in *Bodies of Work* (London, Serpent's Tail, 1997), p. 156, in which Acker defines Colette's "own kingdom, THE PRESBYTERY, her multilanguage of multieverything . . ." This essay is one of the sites where one can discover Acker's strong identification with Colette.
3. Denis Hollier, *Against Architecture: The Writings of Georges Bataille* (Cambridge, MA, MIT Press, 1992), p. xi.

4. *Bodies of Work.*
5. See also Denis Hollier's extensive discussion of the labyrinth of Bataille in *Against Architecture.*
6. See "Realism in the Cause of Future Revolution," in *Bodies of Work*, p. 19.
7. This is the title of an essay in *Bodies of Work.*
8. See the interview with Sylvére Lotringer in *Hannibal Lecter, My Father* (New York, Semiotext(e), 1991) pp. 11–24.
9. Kathy Acker, *My Mother: Demonology* (New York, Grove Press, 1993), p. 206.
10. Ibid., p. 207.
11. Denise Riley, *The Words of Selves: Identification, Solidarity, Irony* (Stanford, CA., Stanford University Press, 2000), p. 156.
12. *Against Architecture*, p. ix.
13. See Kathy Acker, "I Realize Something" and particularly pp. 202–203 of *Empire of the Senseless* (New York, Grove Press, 1988).
14. *Against Architecture*, p. ix.
15. *Empire of the Senseless, p. 227.*
16. Kathy Acker, *Pussy King of the Pirates* (New York, Grove Press, 1996), p. 110.
17. Ibid., p. 110.
18. *Bodies of Work*, pp. 16–17.

The Greatness of Kathy Acker

Robert Glück

Jesus saw some little ones nursing—He said to his disciples, "What these little ones who are nursing resemble is those who enter the kingdom." They said to him, "So shall we enter the kingdom by being little ones?" Jesus said to them, "When you make the two one and make the inside like the outside and the outside like the inside and the above like the below, and that you might make the male and the female be one and the same, so that the male might not be male nor the female be female, when you make eyes in the place of an eye and a hand in place of a hand and a foot in place of a foot, an image in place of an image— then you will enter the kingdom."

The Gospel According to Thomas

I read *I Dreamt I Was a Nymphomaniac*, I think, before I met Kathy Acker or even heard of her. I was snacking on the stock of the poetry bookstore that I co-directed. I could see the book was provocative and experimental, and the sex kept me alert. The second chapter contains a passage that begins, "Last night I dreamt I was standing on a low rise of grassy ground," and continues to describe a dream that involves family, the art world, and sex. Then the next paragraph begins, "Last night I dreamt I was standing on a low rise of grassy ground . . ."[1] I began the second passage with a sense of having been there before, like a dream. Then a dawning sense of wrongness, then certainty of wrongness and a search for an explanation. A printer's error seemed the probable cause. Lord knows, the small-press books in my store contained zillions of mistakes.

I read the second passage more carefully than the first, because if there were any differences between them, I would have the relief of seeing the author making variations, but there were no differences. That made me suffer. Since the second passage duplicated the first, my arousal and emotions were taken from me, and I wanted to hold on to them. "If I don't fuck someone soon, know someone wants me, I'll have to ride my horse for three days again: do something wilder. I can't stop myself. I get another drink. My sister who's also drunk asks me to dance . . . she kisses me . . . I ask her and she says she'd like to fuck me." The dream contains many of Acker's themes, always close at hand in any case: suicide, sex, incest, family money, romance, loneliness, the inhumanity of "this society."

Why were my feelings taken from me by this repetition? Because I no longer knew Acker's reason for telling me the dream. Like any reader, I depend on knowing the author's intention to stabilize my reading, because I use her belief to underwrite the intensities that are generated and modulated inside me. Instead, Acker dispatched these emotions while I was more or less stuck with them. It is a strange loneliness to be abandoned, emotions disowned, choking on the equipment of narrative projection. Acker destabilized my reading by a strange doubling in which I saw how artificial the emotions were—or were made to be—even as I fell into them. They became an example of emotion, quoted emotion, and the effect of her quote marks was to slide me back and forth between embrace and distance. I am describing an aesthetic effect: I was left stranded with story as the writer leaped into the cold heaven of formal abstraction.

Many of Acker's strategies keep the reader off-balance. That's why it's rather difficult to write about her work, because the best reading is an uncertain reading. I want to offer my confusion as an ideal. Rather than drawing conclusions, developing identifications or thematic connections, that is, making judgments that lead to knowledge, Acker creates a reader who is lost in strangeness. She pitches the reader into a welter of contradictions that do not resolve themselves, but replace each other continuously: a text that hates itself but wants me to love it, sex that dissolves and amalgamates, a disempowered self that tops its heated bottom-act with cold manipulations, a confession that is therapeutic without the possibility of health. Her aesthetic is founded on double binds whose brilliance captivates me as I struggle against them.

The dream passage was repeated a third and a fourth time, and I understood how coldly and elegantly the second passage turned the dream into collaged text. By the fourth repeat I was skimming—I had been turned out of the story and saw it as a block of text. Acker's location had gone from the "I" of the dreamer to the manipulator of text. My own location as reader also changed, I was deprived of one kind of identification in favor of another. When Acker applies pressure to modes of narrating, she compels me to stand with her as the writer of her book, perhaps just living with her through a chunk of time: the theme jumps from, say, incest to the materiality of print and the notion that texts themselves can be "represented." I feel a kind of joy as I attain that grander perspective. But that position is continually undermined by the story being told.

Acker says in 1989, in the useful interview that Sylvère Lotringer conducted, "The I became a dead issue because I realized that you make the I and what makes the I are texts."[2] When I lost my purchase as a reader, I felt anguish exactly because I was deprived of one identity-making machine of identification and recognition. I gained my footing on a form of identification that was perhaps more seductive, a second narrative about Acker manipulating text and disrupting identity. To treat a hot subject in a cold way is the kind of revenge that Flaubert took. Acker's second narrative acts as a critical frame where I discover how to read the work: the particular ways in which a marauding narrative continually shifts the ground of authority, subverting faith in the "suspension of disbelief" or guided daydream that describes most fiction. Acker blasts that arrangement wide open by locating the writing in her own life and in the life of the reader and then calling for the reader's disbelief. I read these and other narratives all at once and I am a tag team running from one to another. If identity equals a florescence of narratives, or the materiality of language, I must give up the sense of myself as a coherent narrative, and no matter how sophisticated my reading becomes, that is always a struggle. Hence my suffering.

If we see identity as the ongoing formation of a subject through the subject's ongoing negotiation with power, in Acker's work that negotiation is profoundly lost, because identity itself is a tyranny from above that descends *like a wolf on the fold*, as debased as the society that gives and withholds value. The self/text is at heart a political system, as nasty as the society it is part of. Identity and even subjectivity are prisons, the most intimate expressions of a domination that is almost total. "I feel I feel I feel I have no language, any emotion to me is a prison."[3] Struggle equals gestures that fuck with identity.

The heroines of Acker's novels want sex. Arousal may be a drug—"I've gotten hooked on sex"[4]—but it is also a blissful jailbreak from the confines of the self. It is pleasure happening, not the self. Still, to get sex, a person must appear to be something recognizable—say, a gendered being with "appropriate" emotions. It is a double bind that Acker rejects with a grievance enacted by her narrators and characters. Acker declines to accept the terms of our confinement. She even rejects gender, the form the body takes to get "needs met," and she declines to commit to one or any. "I want to be a baby more than have sex. I would rather go GOOGOO."[5] That is, I want the freedom to have no ego boundaries. If texts and selves are prisons, would it be too fanciful to find a kind of freedom in the non-space between texts, in the silence and emptiness between juxtapositions? Some of us experience this kind of freedom as anguish, but we prisoners might also experience other kinds of freedom as anguish.

Acker takes revenge on power by displaying what it has done; she speaks truth to power by going where the power differential is greatest, to a community of whores, adolescent girls, artists and bums, the outcast and disregarded. The power imbalance itself causes a reversal that confers authority, not to identity—these characters are merely quick sketches—but to the realities of oppression, loss, and degradation. If hegemony defines itself by what it tries to exclude, then the excluded merely need to describe themselves in order to describe hegemony.

In the program where I teach, a student wrote about sex with toddlers and violence with guns. He was unrelenting. When the class he attended closed down, he was sent to work with me. Extra-literary questions swarmed his writing: he worked the nightshift at the sheriffs' office, and he brought his gun to class for show-and-tell. He was in his sixties, so no youthful hi-jinx there. Had he acted—was he going to act—on his imaginings? Was I supposed to regard his writing as abnormal psychology rather than fiction? If so, even a fake confession was part of a true case history. He was a skillful and even funny writer. I found myself laughing—was that complicity? Was the humor intentional? I could picture the front page of *The Chronicle*: Teacher gives A+ to Killer Rapist Paedophile. Intention itself was blown wide open, so his text was in a sense illegible.

I feel again that I was in the position of Acker's ideal reader, just as I had been in the bookstore encountering Acker's work for the first time. By best reader, I mean that I was implicating myself in ways I couldn't foresee. The considerable power I enjoy—that of a professor judging a student's work—was turned upside down because it was myself I had to judge, along with the workings of the very power that kept me safe from the text, and safe generally. If I had read my student's work in a book published by Grove Press, or published by anyone, the scandal might have been contained by the form of its publication, and I would have neutralized the danger rightly or wrongly by placing it in a tradition of transgressive literature. In order to make scandal felt continually, Acker finds ways to overflow the bounds of the literary by combining the knowledge she gives us of her life with aggression, humor, unfairness, and shifts in diction and context. "I asked him if he had gotten a letter from Mother . . . 'Were you expecting the dead to tell you what it's like so you can have a new place to spread your cunt lips?'"[6] Cultural tenets are demolished because I can't contain this damage in the box of literature.

Kathy blabs, but not necessarily the truth. Early on, she mixed real and fake autobiography according to set formulas, as she explains in the interview with Lotringer.[7] She manipulates my urge to build a reality behind an I. I want to believe that her story occurs in the world I inhabit: I'm hooked into her outrageous desires—they must be *real*. But Acker denies me the means to draw a conclusion, a conclusion she is not committed to herself. If this is a performance in writing, what is at stake? Belief in the fact or fiction of events is no longer a pressing issue, because the risk of performing takes its place—if I am not sure of how naked she has made herself, I can still react to the spectacle of "how far will she go." And my risk as a spectator becomes the risk of complicity, that the confessional machinery will somehow get backloaded onto me, that it is my confession in the end. It is my confession because I stage it in my psyche, because it calls a community into being that I am part of, because I already know the story so it is already mine, and because Acker has thoroughly confused belief, doubt, and emptiness.

Acker makes a nether region because she structures extra-literary relationships into her writing, which complicates the kind of judgments most readers never need to make. Finally, judgment itself is worn down and falls away in favor of a kind of astonishment. In this sense, you could say Acker creates extra-literary conflict that does not build character either on the page or in the world, as most fiction intends to do, but instead destroys character.

Acker expanded the range of what can be said about the body, and all who write about sex owe her a debt of gratitude. There's no precedent for her patient records of pleasure, coldly observed. "If I concentrate on the air my lungs draw into themselves, I can feel the nerves around my breasts move and shift in complex patterns."[8] She records consciousness as it moves through the phantasmagoria of daydream and the reality of the body as a first place: "This lasts forever: time intercedes, I can feel his cock expand."[9]

How true the confession and how proximate the complicity that create arousal! Following the lead of Georges Bataille, Acker says that sex destroys limits: "I matter when someone touches me, when I touch someone; the touch matters; so in this way I no longer exist, nor do the men."[10] But there is a contradiction here, because sex is often the place in Acker's writing that recognizable time and space begin. Sometimes Acker borrows from porn—high-class porn by Alexander Trocchi, for example—which has its own time frame of tension and release, and its own characters. But often she is simply looking at sex for a long time. So sex stabilizes the self/text as much as sex destabilizes it. Arousal occurs on a register in which continuity is reinstated. Sex operates as a kind of weather, it takes the place of representation's bric-a-brac. It puts the world in place: here's the "effect of the real." "The hair curling above the cunt, between the thighs, around the outer lips, in the red crack of the ass touches the thick pink outer lips touches the tiny red inner lips inside the outer lips touches the red berry at one end of the inner lips whose inside grows if its grazed lightly enough touches the muscles and nerves spiraling as a canal away from the red inner lips."[11] Acker draws in the reins of all her other preoccupations in favor of close observation.

To present myself as a reader of Acker's sex writing, I include my own extra-literary commitment, both to the body in the form of my arousal and to the community of sexual experimentation that is supported by such writing. Acker's voice describing sex is most often her "real voice"—as she described it—a voice which becomes more present in her later books.

I want to take this sex-equals-stability another step. That we have bodies, and a relation to these bodies, and a lack of relation to these bodies, is politics for Acker. Flesh is what has value. Kathy and I used to trade nuggets of physical experience. Talking on the phone, one of us would say something like, "She can't have an orgasm unless a third person is watching," and the other would pounce on it. We were on the look out for an irreducible language, an irreducible chunk of experience to put together with other irreducible chunks to make a language where feeling, event, and words come together. "I need to fuck guys who fuck really slowly, for a long time, so it just comes over me. I tremble and tremble and tremble."[12] A language that can't exist, in which the most ephemeral is the most enduring. A magical language whose words fasten onto their readers' bodies in a kind of onomatopoetic fury. Sex is a bit like a magic spell, like sympathetic magic: an erection on the page can cause an erection "in the world." Using these nuggets has the same pleasure as correcting the error of generalization, since each one stands for a whole sexuality, a species of one.

Acker's ambition for literature was to site it in a queasy place where autobiography and fiction, politics and myth become indistinguishable. She brings language to its limits, to the body and emotions—where risk of nakedness derives from and supports a community. "Culture's the way by which a community attempts to bring its past up out of senselessness and to find in dream and imagination possibilities for action."[13]

Certainly she stands with Juan Goytisolo and Thomas Bernhard in the pitch of her hatred for her country, for "this society." Against the loneliness of her experience, Acker posits the ongoing conversation of a group of whores that defines community, a gathering of outcasts that evolves into a band of pirates in her final book. They're already present in her first work, "Politics," about her life as a dancer in a strip joint. These gatherings are composed of women, artists, and freaks who review their relationships with men and power on the eternal stage of night and empire, whether it's a New York City jail or imperial Rome. This community draws an equal sign between freeing our ability to love and the destruction of the state. Included in that community is Acker's reader; as she says, "When I use language, I am given meaning and I give meaning back to the community."[14]

In 1975 Acker wrote about "A possibility of living in a world to which she's not always alien. San Francisco!"[15] Acker's move from city to city—New York, San Francisco, London—was the story of hope and disappointment. The demand she placed on the local communities to support her in an unalienated fashion was more interesting for being unreasonable and unfair. Kathy was always on the look out for forms of collectivity—art scenes, music scenes, the tattoo or biker "communities"—that tie the fate of the individual to the fate of the group. In her essay, "Critical Languages," she says: "May we write, not in order to judge, but for and in (I quote Georges Bataille), 'The community of those who do not have a community.'"[16] That is, generating text means generating identity. I would like to add, generating identity means generating community. If the idea of community began so heterogeneously, I wonder if the reductionist pitfalls could be avoided.

Acker included her communities in her writing by using real names, by speaking to them directly, and by speaking for them. "Friendship is always a political act, for it unites citizens into a polis, a (political) community."[17] She loved gossip, the glue of any community, and there was never a greater sob-sister. She does not dress up romantic suffering with pretty language. Love, when it's done right, only makes things worse: "It's sick to love someone beyond rationality, beyond a return (I love you you love me). Real love is sick. I could love death."[18] And, "I knew I belonged to the community of artists or freaks not because the anger in me was unbearable but because my overpowering wish to give myself away wasn't socially acceptable."[19]

Kathy was the best girlfriend, because with her you could really complain. "I am lonely out of my mind. I am miserable out of my mind . . . I've got to fuck. Don't you understand don't you have needs as much as I have needs DON'T YOU HAVE TO GET LAID?"[20] Romantic distress was a default position for human communication, and if the truest language is the unique particulars of desire spoken by the community of cock and cunt, then the lack of such communication (which means no agency, rejection, emotional harm, and poverty) makes a communal language of failure. When I was *badly loved*, no romantic bruise was too tiny to examine, no repeat of that examination was too obsessive. Kathy and I gave each other plenty of advice, the blind leading the blind. Bits of these endless conversations worked their way into each other's writing—here are two tiny passages.

This is from *Great Expectations*, 1982: Three whores are talking in ancient Rome. Kathy is the whore Cynthia, I am the whore Barbarella and Denise Kastan is Danielle.

BARBARELLA: I'm both the wife and husband. Even though none of us is getting anything right now, except Danielle who's getting everything, our desires are totally volatile.
DANIELLE: I can't be a wife. I can be a hostess. If I've got lots of money.
BARBARELLA: One-night stands don't amuse me anymore.
CYNTHIA: I think if you really worship sex, you don't fuck around. Danielle fucks around more than any of us, and she's the one who doesn't care about sex.
BARBARELLA: Most men don't like sex. They like being powerful and when you have good sex you lose all power.
CYNTHIA: I need sex to stay alive.[21]

This is from my book *Margery Kempe* from 1994:

> It's two a.m. his time; I'm in bed in San Francisco. My life occurs on the heavy satin of his skin yet he won't let me be the cause of stimulation. I give him an ultimatum: Let's live together or break up. He thinks it over a few months: he has the self-confidence to reject me. I write a blistering letter and show it to my friend Kathy. She says, "Bob, you must delete the anger and beg."[22]

"One text subverts another" is the consecrated phrase. Appropriation can express a cynicism where nothing obtains ("My writing is all shit," as Kathy once affirmed in P.J.'s, a seafood restaurant in San Francisco), and the process itself can be pitched like a bomb at the custodians of identity. In her hands it's a malleable practice—in her later work Acker uses appropriation to conduct us into a state of wonder. ("I'm basically a New Age writer," Kathy said some years later at the same table.)

Great Expectations begins with episodes of family life alternating with chunks of Acker's translations of Pierre Guyotat's *Eden Eden Eden*, a novel-length sentence fragment on sex and atrocity. Soon the sections infect each other and we see the link between need and violence—that family life and war (in 1982 Guyotat's Algeria looked like our Vietnam) have their common denominator. "*Reality* is just the underlying fantasy, a fantasy that reveals need."[23] Need means need for love on every register. Reality is need in a simpler way than we might be comfortable acknowledging: Acker may be subverting text with text but need has a different economy: one text equals all texts and one need equals all needs. One need is not an allegory of all needs; it is all needs.

Another way to describe this economy of need is to say that appropriation is a way to look at the distance between feeling and event. One of Acker's basic tenets is that the world is against feeling. She projects her life into events that are already known, like porn or detective genre or canonical works like *Don Quixote* and *Great Expectations*. The already-known is a public stage on which to reclaim emotion. It's a theme in *Don Quixote*—how to love while ferociously transvaluing emotion and continuously redefining world and self. In works like *Don Quixote* and *Pussy, King of the Pirates*, appropriation grants Acker's own story a second fate with its own inevitabilities, its own organization of experience. You could say this fate is a fate in words with its own freedoms and resistances. The appropriated text acts as the unforeseen since—once begun—Kathy's life must somehow fit into the story.

The rereading that *is* appropriation turns Acker into a reader as well as a writer. "The more I write my own novels, the more it seems to me that to write is to read."[24] Acker jumps the barrier and becomes a reader—displaying that projection of self into the text that shapes—however briefly—a reader's being. That projection of herself is presented as a kind of spectacle to myself the reader, part of my own act of self-projecting. In reading, I am pitched between the true version of the appropriated work, its theft, the facts of Acker's life, and the truth of her psychic life (the "case history" of extremity that writers since de Quincey have been reporting).

I have come to think of the trajectory of Acker's writing as going from daydream to night dream. In the first place Acker took her cue from early seventies conceptual art, banishing creativity and asserting procedural elements of writing by setting up arbitrary guidelines to set fiction outside intention: in *Kathy Goes to Haiti*, she used predetermined amounts of real and fake autobiography. She wrote so many pages per day, brute production, which she called task work. At one point she said she wrote with the TV on, and bits of histrionic soap-opera dialogue sometimes filtered through. I'll bet boredom induced daydream. Her early work, taken as a whole, can be characterized by daydream, that is, dream riffs of clear motive, immediate longings, revenge fantasies, and wish-fulfillment.

Acker used dreams in many ways—the dream maps in *Blood and Guts* for example. There is a therapeutic aspect to the repetition of the family drama, the litany of obsessions, the report of endless suffering and desire. Writing may provide the same occasion for self-revelation that therapy does—we take for granted that it's good for people to speak candidly in these "confidential" situations. But it is a therapy in which good health is impossible because the dream is turned outward—deprived of interiority, stripped of coherent subjectivity—and it is our culture itself that is sick. The endless recycling of societal messages and oppressions enlarges the sense of impossibility, except perhaps faith in the power of storytelling itself. A therapy minus interior life, anti-expressive, and so turned outward.

In *My Death My Life by Pier Paolo Pasolini* Acker wrote, "I can wonder whatever I want. I simply see. Each detail is a mystery a wonder."[25] Acker was searching for a way to escape from duality and rational thought. In *Empire of the Senseless* she dreamt the plot forward. Acker would make a move in writing, like dreaming a plot forward, then see that she was doing it and make a commitment to the strategy, as Carla Harryman observed at the Lust for Life symposium at New York University in 2002. After *Empire of the Senseless* was finished, she said she was glad to sleep through a night again, since she had been waking herself up for months to write down her dreams. The dreams are recognizable—Kathy moving through a dream space where motive seems emphatic for her and for the reader, though located beyond the grasp of both. Dualities are cancelled in favor of an immediate consciousness of the interrelation and interdependence of things. Acker was using her unconscious like a public commons, the location of image-making that belongs to a community.

I'd like to place Acker's later work with Baudelaire's "Correspondences" and Rimbaud's *Illuminations*, works intended to change the world directly through the reality of the imagination. "If writing cannot and writing must change things, I thought to myself, logically of course, writing *will* change things magically."[26] Acker's interest in magic can be seen as the grandest attempt to integrate the extra-literary into writing. Magic, in the largest sense, allows me to link my own experience, desires, and biological self to a grand order. It connects the ephemeral to the largest reality. Acker uses the emphatic but obscure motives of dreams to indicate this unknown organization of the world. Maybe she is rejecting the idea that anything is secret, so her dreams belong to the reader as well as the writer, and the goal of self-knowledge is turned outward as well. My interior life may be a cultural glue, something organizing me from the outside, something to live up to, like the idea of fidelity in the Middle Ages.

Acker founds her aesthetics on distant poles. On the one hand she champions feeling itself, and on the other she is a cold writer working from formulas that generate text.

Her continual shifts in scale stretch meaning out of shape, as she packs together extreme statements of far-flung lyricism. Belief itself is "bent out of shape," an exciting disorganization that isolates each sentence in an immensity. Acker can inhabit both sides of a cliché. A sentence like "I'm sick of this society" can seem at once post-punk self-mockery, ugly writing shedding the trappings of literature, the stupid voice of an adolescent girl who can't be controlled, an "example of language," and a *cri de cœur*. I must continually renew my trust in the process of reading while my assumptions are demolished. I attain a place of innocence, my affirmation and trust must take place in the present—past affirmations don't matter, past betrayals of that trust must be surmounted. The writing itself gains majesty as, finally, the truth of the world seems to be balanced against each sentence.

Kathy Acker had the highest ambitions: to reorient literature in a true relation to the present and to crack that moment wide open. In the end, my reading goes from unreadable to unbearable, because Acker intends that I bear the knowledge of chance, which is the acceptance of constant change. That acceptance is also the knowledge of death, the knowledge of my body which exists (whether I know it or not) in the pure intensity of arousal and dread.

Notes

1. Kathy Acker, *I Dreamt I Was a Nymphomaniac: Imagining*, in *Portrait of an Eye: Three Novels* (New York, Grove Press, 1998), pp. 101–102.
2. "Devoured by Myths" (interview), in *Hannibal Lecter, My Father* (New York, Semiotext(e), 1991), p. 11.
3. *Great Expectations* (San Francisco, Re/Search, 1982), p. 24.
4. *Hello, I'm Erica Jong* in *Essential Acker* (New York, Grove Press, 2002), p. 149.
5. Ibid., p. 148.
6. *In Memoriam to Identity* (New York, Grove Weidenfeld, 1990), p. 165.
7. *Hannibal Lecter,* "Interview," p. 7.
8. *The Childlike Life of the Black Tarantula*, in *Portrait of an Eye*, pp. 59–60.
9. *Rip-off Red, Girl Detective* (New York, Grove Press, 2002), p. 11.
10. *The Childlike Life*, in *Portrait of an Eye*, p. 53.
11. *The Adult Life of Toulouse Lautrec*, in *Portrait of an Eye*, p. 53.
12. Ibid., pp. 202–203.
13. "On Art and Artists," *Bodies of Work*, (London, Serpent's Tail, 1997), p. 4.
14. Ibid., 4.
15. *The Adult Life of Toulouse Lautrec,* in *Portrait of an Eye*, p. 208.
16. "Critical Languages (1990)" in *Bodies of Work*, p. 92.
17. "Writing, Identity, and Copyright in the Net Age," in *Bodies of Work*, p. 104.
18. *My Mother: Demonology* (New York, Pantheon Books, 1993), p. 15.
19. *Don Quixote*, in *Essential Acker*, p. 212.
20. "New York City in 1979," in *Essential Acker*, p. 139.
21. *Great Expectations*, p. 110.

22. Robert Glück, *Margery Kempe* (New York/London, Serpent's Tail, 1994), p. 134.
23. *Blood and Guts in High School*, in *Essential Acker*, p. 115.
24. "The Words to Say It," in *Bodies of Work*, p. 66.
25. *My Death My Life by Pier Paolo Pasolini*, in *Essential Acker*, p. 195.
26. "A Few Notes on Two of my Books," in *Bodies of Work*, p. 8.

Foucault Reads Acker
and Rewrites the History of the Novel

Barrett Watten

> When I was first introduced to the work of Foucault [. . .] it was very political; it was about what was happening to the economy and about changing the political system. By the time it was taken up by the American academy, the politics had gone to hell. It became an exercise for some professors to make their careers.
>
> Kathy Acker[1]

It is often forgotten that Michel Foucault early in his career was a reader of the avant-garde, specifically of Artaud, Bataille, Roussel, Sade, and others. And it has not sufficiently been observed that central insights gained from that study led directly to his formulations of madness, discursive subjectivity, the archive, and genealogy. As a project of historical investigation, Foucault's recovery of the documentary narrative of *I, Pierre Rivière* . . . discloses a relation between narrative form, madness, and law that directly anticipates the form of Kathy Acker's writings. What if Foucault had continued to be interested in literary readings, and to factor into his genealogy of discourse the negativity of the avant-garde? Such an inquiry might have led Foucault back to the question of genre in literature, specifically the novel, which constructs social discourse as much as it is constituted by it. Kathy Acker's contribution to the genre, in this light, would be a significant moment of avant-garde decomposition of genre into its textual and experiential components.[2] If Foucault were to read Acker and rewrite the history of the novel, I propose, its genealogy would in his view not originate with the propriety of *Pamela*'s virtue but descend from the criminality and sexuality of *Moll Flanders*. Triangulating Acker's work between *Moll Flanders* and *Pierre Rivière* allows one to disclose her formal motives, which are to undo and reinvent the novel as an inversion of the historical crisis of its negative, excessive origins.

Avant-Garde Foucault

There is a secret history in the writings of Foucault: his use of the avant-garde. While it briefly appears in his biography, it is hardly addressed in his intellectual history, and this is especially true of his American reception.[3] Academic uses of Foucault, from new historicism to queer theory, tend as a matter of procedure to limit his central concept of discourse to a rhetoric of bounded inquiry within discursive (institutional/academic) frames, tending toward a pseudo-positivist normativity that severs the historical provocation and liberationist goals of the avant-garde from Foucault's total project. A re-encounter with the negativity of Foucault's avant-garde sources is long overdue, one taking into account his early book on Raymond Roussel;[4] his many references to Sade, Bataille, and Artaud; and the postwar European avant-garde represented in journals such as *Tel Quel* in the 1960s.[5] The institutional/academic privileging of the normative and socially regulative, to the extent that it partakes of Foucault's accounts of the prison and sexuality, fails to comprehend the constitutive negativity that is distributed everywhere in his work, one of whose original sources is the avant-garde. Madness, death, and eroticism are the key elements of the discursive epistemes that Foucault investigates in the asylum, archive, and clinic; without Sadean destruction there would be no going beyond the author and no genealogy. For Foucault, the way the radical forms and social positions of the avant-garde disclose the incoherence of culture anticipates the way madness, death, and sexuality pervade the regularities of knowledge and experience. A rereading of Foucault after Kathy Acker, then, would restore an originary encounter that had been passed over.

A Foucauldian avant-garde would recover the negativity distributed in discourse, by undoing the "regularity in dispersion" that binds together the discourses we live over long durations.[6] If dispersion, as a species of negativity, is an entailment of regularity and the construction of norms, then the avant-garde may be something other than what we thought it was; perhaps it does not historically originate in a series of aesthetic examples from Baudelaire, Manet, to dada but repeats as a discontinuous moment of recursive breakdown and social reflexivity.[7] Such a revised avant-garde would be the "becoming outside" of the system as it reflects on itself and rejects what it sees, looking for a higher, unknowable wholeness to replace the false totality of the historical present.[8] The systemic negativity that results would then be distributed in the spatial form of the avant-garde as a positive phenomenon, as a discontinuous social matrix of movements, groups, and subcultures.[9] The spatial and temporal negativity of the avant-garde—its dislocation within a culture in which it finds itself as other—inverts the formation of discursive regularities in temporal and spatial senses, leading to their epistemic dismantling and reformation. But rather than reifying a single, strained negative dialectics in which avant-garde agency performs a permanent refusal of integration—one that is good for philosophy as well—we need to keep open the spontaneity, instability, and evanescence of the avant-garde as a negative element within the sutured construction of discourse. The question of the avant-garde concerns the social distribution and historical specificity of the negative—not simply an oppositional moment but a destructive/renewing one of systemic de-totalization.[10]

Foucault has been accurately seen as writing against any teleological sublation of negativity after Hegel: how then does he position the negativity of the avant-garde? He does so precisely in seeing negativity, avant-garde or otherwise, as nonteleological. In a key citation of Artaud in *Madness and Civilization*, Foucault hypothesizes a mutually constitutive exclusion of the artistic work and madness: "Madness is the absolute break with the work of art; it forms the constitutive moment of abolition, which dissolves in time the truth of the work of art; it draws the exterior edge, the line of dissolution, the contour against the void."[11] At the same time, the coincidence of madness with the "final instant" of the work returns us to its truth: "The moment when, together, the work of art and madness are born and fulfilled is the beginning of the time when the world finds itself arraigned by that work of art and responsible before it for what it is" (ibid., 289).[12] This claim for the coincidence of negativity and the truth of art—very likely a direct influence of Heidegger on Foucault—makes sense, in turn, of the radical antiformalism, the identity of limit experiences with form, that will enable the latter's linking of Sade, Bataille, and Roussel.[13] In each, the systematic regularities of the work make possible its potential truth in a co-determination and shattering of limits. So the repeated litany of bodily destruction in Sade, constructing regularity in the violation of natural law, leads to the practice of knowledge in the medical clinic, where the regular opening-up of bodies becomes a structuring principle of knowledge. Just so, in the genealogy of Foucault's work, insights gained from works of art, especially radically antiformalist ones, cede to the dispersed regularity of practices, discourses, and epistemes. It makes sense, though, that Foucault would go beyond aesthetic examples once he had shown them as constituted in the undoing of limits. We may well ask under what circumstances Foucault, had he lived, would have returned to questions of artistic form, once he had gone "beyond" them in the early 1970s, with his work on the prison and sexuality—at about the same time Acker was undertaking a radical revision of the novel as discourse, as we will see.

London, 1722

Let us imagine a revisionist genealogy of the novel after Foucault.[14] What would such an account look like? If kept to the English tradition, it might well have descended from the example of Daniel Defoe's *Moll Flanders*—a significant counterclaim, in that *Moll Flanders* has an honorable place in literary history as being the *one* work that fails, in terms of numerous criteria, to inaugurate the history of the English novel. At the top of a litany of objections for traditional critics, *Moll* is accused of a failure in the coherence of narrative voice, indulging a kind of flattening of affect that prevents sustained belief in the protensions and retensions of the character's continuity in time.[15] The narrative does not really seem to develop at all, but is always returning to a kind of abstract inventory of Moll's fortunes that is framed as a series of entertaining but inconclusive episodes. There are numerous anachronisms or errors that threaten the spatio-temporal unity of the work as well, and a colossal failure of motivation when, having committed every crime short of murder and having overturned every conventional moral perspective that founds the values of the narrative, Moll is rewarded with a fortune at the end. As a character, Moll is a persistent liar, and the reader's identification with her is always on unstable ground, between an incredulity based on factual manipulation or the pleasure gained from fictional disavowal. Finally, the novel as fiction evinces the cardinal sin that will decisively remove it from consideration as the inaugural form of the genre: it "bleeds into history," refusing to entirely transform its documentary sources into a fully realized aesthetic work of moral reflection.[16] In this "bleed into history," the identity of the author as much as the heroine is in doubt, considering the numerous textual and ideological complications of Defoe's work. Defoe both denied authorship of works known to be written by him and claimed authorship of works he did not write; embroiled in both political and copyright disputes, he had many reasons to evade authorial responsibility.[17] All these failures explain why Foucault would begin his genealogy of the novel with Moll Flanders, and further why such a genealogy could easily be extended to include Acker.[18] *Moll's* duplicity and instability, her lack of personal identity, provides an obvious touchstone for Acker's work, as her early use of the history of London cutthroats similar to Defoe's, and her later explicit borrowings from that tradition in *Pussy, King of the Pirates*, clearly acknowledges.[19]

Moll Flanders as a surrogate type of the emergence of the novel in its descent to Acker provides a good example of what Foucault means by genealogy: a dissociative play on positive knowledge that widens the gap between narrative and event.[20] Such a genealogical undermining of narrative and event is precisely what Foucault undertakes in the historical construction of *I, Pierre Rivière, having slaughtered my mother, my sister, and my brother . . .*[21] On the grand scale of sociopathology, Rivière's account of his multiple murders reaches the final instant in which the work locates its truth in the world at the limit of its unaccountability. His testimony entails, like the avant-garde, a becoming outside of the system as it reflects on itself and rejects what it sees, looking for a higher, unknowable wholeness to replace the false totality of the historical present—but from the perspective of a sociopath trying to exploit gaps in the legal discourse that will judge him. For Foucault, this is neither tragedy nor farce but a construction of knowledge that takes into account Pierre's (and the legal system's) necessarily inadequate answer to the law's demand for disclosure of the truth of the event. Such a discursive construction depends on a fundamental dissociation that frames the negativity of the event: the narrative of Rivière's multiple murders could only be written by him *after* the event had taken place, even as he claims to have formulated it as a script for the performance *before* the event. There is a dissociation as well of the knowledge of madness in the text: Rivière deceptively constructs, in an apparently rational way, a series of motivational gaps in the narrative that would prove he is mad; the claim that his crime was an act of madness allows him a plausible defense of it in and as its rationalization at the (later) time of judgment. It is here that Rivière's narrative leaves the formal coherence of narrative as it "bleeds into history": just so, Foucault's research group surrounds the core confession with a series of historical documents, including their own analyses, as corroborating elements of the work's madness. Madness and the legal system of documentation are seen as fundamentally intertwined in this construction of discourse, in such a way that interior motivation and external judgment align. Negativity is distributed in structures that finally determine narrative motives—Rivière's, the French legal system's, and finally those of Foucault's group—at the constitutive limits of discourse. As long as such gaps between these discursive elements remain open, we are in the domain of construction and may avoid the false positives of history; this is how genealogy keeps the inaccessible moment of event open through a play of negativity that at the same time constitutes discourse and judgment.

It is legitimate to question here the nature of this avoidance: if we refuse all positivity (of personal identity or event), on what possible basis can we make a judgment or write a narrative? This paradox has been identified as Foucault's "rejectionism" (in *I, Pierre Rivière*, an entailment of his use of multiple perspectives for truth); as one critic put it, "The reading of Foucault as a normative rejectionist of humanism pushes us to choose between a known ethical paradigm and an unknown x."[22] Such an "unknown x" would be precisely Moll's or Rivière's intentional states, the incoherence of their personal identity, in their acts such that they enter a scene of judgment—of either novel or legal discourse—that would determine them. What links Foucault's critical perspectives to the history of novelistic devices from Defoe to Acker is the way in which rejection of known ethical paradigms is necessary for knowledge of an unknown x, given the incompletion of a personal identity that "bleeds into history." If there is any hope for knowledge, it requires us not to leave the scene of the crime, which expands outward to the limits of a form (theory, legal dossier, or novel). This is the effect Foucault pursued in the avant-garde, never better stated than in his account of the formal devices of Georges Bataille, "in the constant movement to different levels of speech and a systematic disengagement from the 'I' [. . .]; temporal disengagements [. . .]; shifts in the distance separating a speaker from his words [. . .]; an inner detachment from the assumed sovereignty of thought or writing." What results is an "exact reversal" of the tradition of personal identity from Socrates on:

It is at the center of the philosophical subject's disappearance that philosophical language proceeds as if through a labyrinth, not to recapture him,
but to test (and through language itself) the extremity of its loss. That is, it
proceeds to the limit and to this opening where its being surges forth, but
where it is already lost, completely overflowing itself, emptied of itself to the
point where it becomes an absolute void . . . This play of transgression and
being is fundamental for the constitution of philosophical language, which
reproduces and undoubtedly produces it. (80)

Theory, criminal confession, and by extension the novel each accomplish, through
the act of transgression, an expansion of limits—the scene of a crime that can
never be left.

Such a refusal to leave the scene of the crime in order not to accept the finality
of judgment is everywhere a formal figure in Acker's work, aligning it with the
narratives of Moll and Rivière and thus making it Foucauldian. Acker's mechanical
copying and transgressive overwriting of unrelated texts creates an "as if"
scenario in which known ethical paradigms and narrative outcomes are rejected
and where plausible or implausible alternatives proliferate as textual play. In so
doing, each of her scenarios' inadequacies constructs a space of madness as
potential/deferred freedom that accedes to knowledge—if only she can keep on
writing long enough for their partial truths to be revealed. Acker's rejection is not
simply a refusal to make sense of herself but to answer to the question of identity
as if it were put to her by a judgment yet to be disclosed, one that requires endless
further elaborations to account for her theft as narrative. Rejecting the continuity
of personal identity, the protension and retention of self and object that founds the
genre of the novel, she substitutes in its place a mode of discontinuous answering
back. The center of Acker's strategies, then, is a dissociation of personal identity
that generates the form of the narrative. Throughout her work, she locates this
dissociation as both blindspot and origin of fiction (much like the cunning of
Pierre Rivière, whose reason is precisely his madness), as in the following from *I
Dreamt I Was a Nymphomaniac: Imagining*:

If by "substance" I mean an individual who exists (continues) without
change and totally independently, I'm not a "substance." Change (temporal
relations) is a substance. If I'm not a substance and yet am a subject, I'm an

individual or a number of individuals. An individual happens only within a present duration; an individual doesn't change. Therefore I'm composed of an unknown number of such individuals. I is a (predicate) relation. (138)

The "unknown x" here is precisely "change," seen as a temporal gap between "individuals" who are durationless and merely present (and not from a perspective outside the present, as for example through narrative closure). "I," therefore, is either an endless series of such individuals or is the substance of temporality itself. This substance cannot be known as the experience of being an individual(s); outside such knowledge, it generates fiction. In a descent from personal identity *as* narrative, Acker's work bleeds into history as "change."

Throughout her work, then, Acker poses a question to *the world* as the limit of coherence—the limit in which the work of art, in Foucault's account of Bataille, cedes to madness as it is determined by the world, rather than any internal motivations that would reflect a continuity of personal identity. If Acker's refusal as a response to interrogation and Foucault's positioning of madness as a "final instant" of the work are conjoined, the larger ethical stakes of rejection may be discerned. The limit of the work of art as refusal is always an answer to the demand for judgment in a world that is subject to change. History begins as the response to a demand: What do you want from me?, where the question is beyond any possibility of response. Foucault's abandonment of the work of art para-doxically leaves open the place of a proper answer to that question: it is in the final instance of the work to answer back. Overwriting a former concern with decision in the work, Foucault turned to the positivity of ethics in the Stoic tradition. While his choice would be to substitute a narrative of "care of the self " for the undecidable work, Acker's adherence to the work continued to answer to the demand of history, but in an improper way. Refusing any ethical norm, it could only present a shifting substitution of selves as its answer to the demand for judgment. Foucault's return to the scene of Acker's writing would be to take up this neglected alternative, thus absolving him of the charge of mere rejectionism, in returning to the scene of decision of the work that he had left behind. Constructing a narrative or work of art as test of history would have definite advantages over the ethical positivity he claimed (and Americans accepted) as the care of the self.[23]

San Francisco, 1973

It is San Francisco, 1973: a number of experimental writers and artists who either will or will not have a great deal to do with one another end up in San Francisco. The first series of Acker's early experimental novels—from *The Childlike Life of the Black Tarantula* to *I Dreamt I Was a Nymphomaniac: Imagining* and *The Adult Life of Toulouse Lautrec by Henri Toulouse Lautrec*[24]—coincides with an eruption of experimental writing, conceptual art, and political poetry. Apart from this scene of literary emergence, the politics of the moment are oppressive, fragmented, and suffused with dread. The Vietnam War continues, an endless stalemate of fake diplomacy and continued mayhem beyond the capacity of oppositional movements to affect an outcome; the utopian counterculture hits the streets of a society with no imaginative appeal and no place for them; the world economy is mired in a global recession caused by skyrocketing oil prices and a combined effect of stagnating production in the industrial democracies.[25] After the convulsive events of the 1960s, repetition and redundancy rear their ugly heads; the mutual dislike of radical utopians and technocrats sets in. In San Francisco, sporadic episodes of violence (the Zodiac killer, the Symbionese Liberation Army [SLA], as later Jonestown and the Moscone/Milk murders) alternate with lines of cars at the gas pumps. Kathy arrives, begins self-publishing. Chapters of *I Dreamed I Was a Nymphomaniac: Imagining* appear in the mail, while in Oakland the depraved logo of the SLA begins show up on public walls.

As experiments in reconstituting the novel, Acker's early texts leave the series of formal examples (particularly in *Black Tarantula*) and initiate their "bleed into history." She thus shifted early from experimental writing as critique of genre to the time of public events, the exterior occasions that define the negativity of the historical moment; Acker's move from public events to the discontinuity of inner life was there from the start. The following chronology of the rise and destruction of the Symbionese Liberation Army provides a ready-to-hand index to the period, easily discernible in both form and content of Acker's writing: "Fall 1973: The Symbionese Liberation Army is formed. Initially a disorganized group of Berkeley student radicals led by ex-convict Donald DeFreeze, it soon develops into a paramilitary organization. Its motto is 'Death to the fascist insect that preys upon the life of the people.'"[26] Acker's early work reflects the paranoia of such formulations, but her identification of these events goes far beyond stylistic fascination. "In the early 1970s, there was escalating violence in California prisons between black inmates and white prison guards. In the Bay Area, white radicals, many of whom lived and studied in Berkeley, began visiting prisoners and sitting in on prison-sanctioned discussion groups." In Marin County, language poet Ron Silliman is performing conscientious objector service for the Committee for Prisoner Humanity and Justice (CPHJ); later he will lobby for legislation to overturn California's indeterminate sentencing laws (and also become an unwilling source of transgressive narration in Acker's mock-porno writings). The political concern with prison reform will find its reference in a series of events, from the prison murder of George Jackson to the Attica revolt. "Through spectacular crimes and their attendant press coverage, the dozen or so founding members of the SLA sought to ignite a 'people's rebellion' against the U.S. government and corporate America. Two months after being kidnapped from a Berkeley apartment, Patty Hearst sends an audiotape to her parents saying she has decided to join the SLA and adopt the name 'Tania.'" Acker was fascinated by the events of the SLA and the figure of Patty Hearst; with the musician Peter Gordon, she recorded two audiotapes titled "Greetings from the SLA," based on Symbionese Liberation Army Communiqué no. 8, May 1974.[27] These events—composites of history and fantasy—would become models for Acker's experiments in the novel, much as various histories of cutpurses were sources for Defoe's *Moll Flanders*.

As liminal subject of history, Hearst provides a central model for Acker's account of the discontinuity of narrative as construction of identity. In a key passage in the chapter titled "I Find an Object for My Desire," she mixes accounts of the SLA with bisexual fantasies of her relationship with Peter Gordon, mapped onto the drama of Patty Hearst:

As a poet I'm actually an agent for the SLA. My mission is to reveal the uncertainties, unimportances, and final equivalences of all identities. Transformation to what? What changes are necessary will occur despite fear and greed. I'm not interested in being a hero . . . I have to pretend I'm in love with Peter . . . / I have to decide whether I'm an SLA agent or a woman transvestite who's wildly in love with the most gorgeous fag in town.

Obviously I'm a woman transvestite who's wildly in love with the most gorgeous fag in town . . . I ask Peter to dance with me. She quivers, moves slightly away from me . . .

"I've never really had a home," she murmurs, "I'm very naïve. I've been carefully guarded all my life, so know nothing of the real and despairing world. I'll never starve or die of bad medical care, for I can always rely on my parents for financial help, but I hate this society: its bases of money and power desires. Every night I dream I'm a member of the SLA I'm hiding from the police I can't figure where to hide. I don't know how most people exist, for they don't have parents like mine."

"I once worked in a sex show," I whispered . . . [Acker:] "Do you believe in marriage?"

[Peter:] "I'd never do thoughtfully anything this society approved of. I admire Tania, Yolanda, Teko, Cujo, Zoya, the others who were willing some did lay down their lives for their vision. I wish I had their courage." (*I Dreamt I Was a Nymphomaniac: Imagining*, 112–114)

This is a definitive passage of both fantasy and narrative construction in the text, uniting the two as its response to the disturbance of actual historical events. In a hybrid fantasy, Acker becomes a masquerading male seducing Peter as transvestite pseudo—Patty Hearst, in the process projecting a significant amount of her psychic material onto him. It is one of a series of payoff moments in her narrative, preceded by a sequence of formal decisions that negotiate the form of narration in terms of privileged areas of content. Acker sets up this possibility of narrative transformation of history by creating a "carrier frequency" of erotic fantasy as the vehicle for the work, as in the first chapter (titled "Desire Begins"): "I absolutely love to fuck. These longings, unexplainable longings within me, drive me wild, and I have no way of relieving them. Living them" (95). Hardly a moment of personal confession, this opening could equally as well be scripted from available soft-core porn sources; the "I" is suspended between a disclosure of actual desire and its concealment in slavish imitation. "My name is Kathy Acker" thus becomes the generic construction of a vehicle for fantasy, having no content of its own: "The story begins by me being totally bored" (96). Acker is quick to acknowledge the motivation for this "I" as construction of the gap between objectless desire and contingent event: "I had no background. I'm not giving you details about myself because these [. . .] occurrences are the first events of my life. Otherwise I don't exist: I'm a mirror for beauty. The man walked up to me and sat down. He bought two beers. I wasn't noticing him" (99). After a boilerplate account of sex with this man, Acker comes to a first definition of her narrative intentions—not to report events but to transform them in fantasy that will lead to the realization of desire: "I want to make something beautiful: an old-fashioned wish. To do this I must first accomplish four tasks, for the last one I must die. Then I'll have something beautiful, and can fuck the men I want because they'll want to fuck me" (101). What follows is a (hardly Proppian) account of the four tasks she must fulfill—an almost word-for-word repetition, four times, of one extended but unmotivated dream, an account that breaks off each time: "As we're fucking, her boyfriend enters the room and stops us because we're not supposed to act soooo" (103, 105, 107, 109). Writing breaks off at the moment the event (here, a dream) becomes so multiply overdetermined that it precludes narration; Acker's task in what follows will be to align, thus, the empty literalness of repeated narration with the overdetermined pressures on identity that cause it to break off and become reconfigured. This is exactly the "bleed into history" where text is exceeded *as* narrative, so that the history produced by the text (not recorded) will be one where "I can fuck the men I want."

The next chapter, taking up the results of the first, purports to "find an object for my desire": Peter Gordon as composite object of personal history and fantasy. "I'm in love with Peter, a man who is capable of deceiving both sexes. He usually wears the clothes of women: long white silk skirts with thin nets of white and snow shawls: in them he looks both like a female faun and like a young boy who adores to tease. / Although Peter is a male, I don't regard his gender as a defect" (111). This indeterminacy of gender precisely is the point where the historical fantasy of Patty Hearst and the SLA enters the text, as a result of the following series: "I'm a poet and what I do is sacred"; "Despite the fact that he didn't choose his sex, I don't dislike men"; and "As a poet I'm actually an agent for the SLA" (110–111).

Being an agent for the SLA—a fantasmatic construction of the Real—is the condition of possibility of gender, which must be similarly split between fantasy and the Real if it is not to be overwhelming and destructive. The empty fantasy of the first chapter, of a nonexistent nymphomaniac writing repetitious dream material, can now be configured around an object—but one constructed by the dissociated method of writing. Just as Pierre Rivière conflates reason and madness, so Acker brings together narration and gender, but only in the possibility that resulting identity is a disrupted construction. The narrative of shifting identifications that follows, of Acker's (non)identity as agent of the SLA, works through numerous fantasies in and around her relation to Peter, finally ending (before the entire passage repeats) in an impossible account of identity as substitution for the multiple personae and unmotivated sequences in which it is embedded:

> There are three kinds of change. Start with a present (a present time interval). Take Peter and me as the individuals in this present: (1) Peter precedes me; or I precede Peter. (2) Peter and I occur together; and Peter disappears, I remain. (3) Peter only: Peter moves, changes color, etc. Or me only: I move, change color, etc. A present duration supposedly means no change. Consider (2). In (2), Peter's and my duration overlap: overlapping is the essence of duration. Because duration must be more complicated than (1) which can be presented by a series of dots on a time line. (3) is continuity: (2) and (3) are the ingredients of duration (or of the present). Apply this notion of duration to another individual: that of identity. My identity at any time depends on (my) lacks of stabilities. (117–118, 125, 137–138)

In this philosophical pastiche, likely adapted from the account of temporality in *Being and Nothingness* (but substituting "Peter" for Sartre's "Paul" as the other who as absent or present does or does not coincide with me), Acker sees personal identity not as protension and retention in a temporal continuity but as a coincidence of substitute identities.[28] This overlap occurs on a time line that is either historical ("before and after," case 1) or durational (an object persists through time; case 3). What interests Acker most is the momentary coinciding of "Peter and I" in case 2, a historical event that makes possible the present tense of an otherwise unstable identity. Paul Ricoeur, in his account of personal identity as narrative construction of sameness (*idem*) and subject (*ipse*), offers a reading of the problematic "coincidence" between Acker and Peter as defining identity in terms of "a specific mediator between the pole of character, where *idem* and *ipse* tend to coincide, and the pole of self-maintenance, where selfhood frees itself from sameness."[29] The character "Peter" thus offers the possibility of a coincidence between duration and self that defines identity—importantly, in a way that history cannot—but it is also one that must be gone beyond as "self-maintenance," or in Acker's terms a renewal of desire. Desire and its object are thus in direct opposition; this is the moment in which the fantasy of history enters into the text, and the Peter/Acker dyad is replaced by Patty Hearst as nonidentical subject of history. Acker's identity occurs in the moment of its identification with/ alienation from the kidnapped heiress as her transvestite lover, an evanescent moment of unstable identity. Identity for Acker is being configured as the impossible temporal coincidence with an other at a historical moment, an other that is at the same time so threatening that it necessitates its own dissolution if the self is to be preserved.

It is not simply that identity is an other; identity is an impossible historical event of coincidence and undoing. In the "real" event that led to this fantasy narrative, Patty Hearst is kidnapped, transforms her identity to Tania, and enacts repressed sexual/revolutionary fantasies on the historical stage. In transforming this story into the register of her own continuous fantasy, Acker's identification with Tania is enacted in the switching of sexual roles between the narrator and Peter. The historical fact of Tania's performance of revolutionary desire (and its sexual component in her imagined relationship with the black revolutionary) is imitated by the swapping of identities across gender boundaries between Acker and Peter. After the Patty Hearst/Tania melodrama, liberation and identity are incompatible for Acker as a historical fact; liberation releases us from stable identity at a moment of destructive convergence, a moment Acker wishes to perpetuate in her writing. Revolution is trauma insofar as it disrupts identity, and the site for this opening is precisely the "wound" of liberation. It is the place where liberation is demanded and turned back as threat, internalized as incomplete—but realized in the fantasmatic gap between self and other, desire and impossible object. For Acker, sexuality and death, a negative eroticism, reveals the breach in the system that records the demand for liberation; her eroticism is the need for destruction of its self and other as unfulfilled demands. This has implications for the narrative form of *I Dreamt I Was a*

Nymphomaniac: Imagining as it continues to work the gap between self and other as the wound of history. In the next chapter, Acker continues a pseudo-historical narrative of Peter as a discontinuous construction of the text: "I found stealing was an addition . . . I can only describe what I now perceived as colors . . . I found that the awareness I had when drunk I could no longer have when sober . . . I became two people. I now think the worst disease of our time is schizophrenia" (132–133). Peter's discontinuity here is his construction, which is underscored by a return to the meditation on the temporal coincidence of identity: " 'I change.' What do I mean by 'I'? . . . By 'I,' I mean an unknown number of individuals. Each individual exists for a present duration and exemplifies one or more characters. These characters exist out of time" (136–137). Here, the dissociation of identity is equal to the permanence of "change," leading to a series of transformations of fantasy material as the novel progresses toward its provisional end. The "unknown number of individuals" who have entered into the text and have been transformed by it turn out to be nameless subjects of liberation in the last chapter, which begins with a consummation of sex with Patty Hearst and ends with a pastiche of Acker's friends in the indeterminate sentences of the California prison system. For liberation, closure only exists as a renewed threat.

Sexuality is the bleed into history that disrupts the temporal continuity of identity likewise for Foucault. But at the same time, Foucault was caught up in political events, not only in fantasy structures but as a public intellectual. Here one can imagine a photograph of Foucault leading a demonstration, arm in arm with Sartre and Genet, marching to the halls of justice. Even so, the bleed into history had its effects on Foucault's work in the early 1970s. In May 1968, Foucault was in Tunisia, finishing up *The Archaeology of Knowledge*, a work that culminates the formal insights he gained from the avant-garde. The shift to historical genealogy took place after the lived experience of change brought on by the events of May 1968.[30] *Pierre Rivière* follows; Rivière's confession is historical in the way that identity can now only be seen as caught in a chiasmus between the (dis)continuity of experience and a historical record determined by institutions. The collective event of *Pierre Rivière*—its postauthorial construction—undoes identity in a text deliberately written as a historical coincidence. There is thus a common project of the undoing of identity in a form of identification that unites Foucault's recovery of Pierre Rivière and Acker's fascination with Patty Hearst. Identity exists only in the disclosure of an event.

Liberationist Acker

For Foucault, what would position *Moll Flanders* in the genealogy of the novel that leads to Acker is the historical coincidence of substitute identities. Moll's novel is the narrative of all the identities she has taken on, as a discursive formation. Motivation is equivalent to a historical coincidence. "I was not the person who took the jewels, now that I have repented," Moll sighs in Newgate Prison; "but our stories do coincide," she admits. This is an insight Foucault could not have had when his investigation into the transgression of identity was confined to the literary series; only after the investigation into the discursive construction of identities could he have formulated the question in this way. Further, it is only after dissociation of identity is given a political dimension in 1968 that Foucault sees the fate of liberationist politics as a construction of institutional forms. If the care of the self is the diminished program that results, a historical return to the question of liberation might have led Foucault to a renewed interest in literature that he had left behind.[31]

For Acker, the bleed into history occurs with the wound of liberation. It is for this reason that opening identity to its arbitrary coincidence with a historical event must be aligned with sexuality. Sexuality is not necessarily liberation in Acker; rather, it is the energetic disturbance of a wound and an attempt to repair it. Acker's interest in literary pastiche and repetition begins here: with the disturbance of identity occasioned by a historical event. In the event, identity is dissociated and revealed; Acker continues to write the event. More precisely, Acker continues to look at writing as the dissolution of an event within a structure that can heal it. Her continued desire for the dissolution of identity—of literary coherence, a stable canon of works, of a consistent address—begins here, with the trauma of an event in which identity could only be seen as a interruption of history.

Acker's method of continuing to seek the dissolution of identity as narrative form may be compared to a parallel negotiation of history, the confession of Patty Hearst. As with Pierre Rivière, we can never know her original motivation in her legitimate account:

> Most of the time I was with them, my mind was going through doing exactly what I was supposed to do. Even if I weren't told, I had been educated very well in what to do. I had been, you know, held in the closet for two months and, you know, abused in all manner of ways. I was very good at doing what I was told.
>
> I had no free will. I had virtually no free will until I was separated from them for about two weeks. And then it suddenly, slowly began to dawn that they just weren't there any more. I could actually think my own thoughts. It was considered wrong for me to think about my family. And when Cinque was around, he didn't want me thinking about rescue because he thought that brain waves could be read or that they'd get a psychic in to find me. And I was afraid of that.[32]

Hearst's narrative provides the restoration in fantasy needed to heal the trauma she had undergone while a member of the SLA. At the same time, the revolutionary and sexual desires she expressed in the event did occur; she *was* "Tania." The dissociation of identity takes place for her—as for Pierre Rivière and Acker's fantasy characters—at a discontinuous moment where it may only, in identification, "coincide." Acker's identification with Hearst shows precisely how the "bleed into history" takes place as an undoing of self that requires further narration. As avant-garde work, her writing shows how "a politics of systemic de-totalization may result when destabilized identity emerges and descends from discursive normativity." As a liberationist text, it records an undoing of self at a historical moment of political crisis that Acker wishes to perpetuate by textual means. Foucault's genealogy of the novel would recognize this, as it rediscovers its sources in Acker and the avant-garde—for which *Moll Flanders* would provide the necessary missing link.

Notes

1. Ellen G. Friedman, "A Conversation with Kathy Acker, *Review of Contemporary Fiction* 9.3 (Fall 1989); available at http://www.centerforbookculture.org/interviews/interview_acker.html.
2. Acker has been described as essentially a poet who wrote novels (as she was by Liz Kotz and David Antin at the Lust for Life symposium at New York Universtiy in 2002). However, in my view, though associated with and inspired by the full range of twentieth-century American poetry, Acker emerges from the tradition of the English novel, and her formal innovations are generically novelistic. Perhaps it may best be said that Acker's work exists at a moment of destruction and renewal between two genres, the novel and poetry, and that her work directly engages questions of genre that are assumed and naturalized in the novel and ignored or denied in poetry.
3. The avant-garde is without question suppressed in the best-known American account of Foucault, Hubert L. Dreyfuss and Paul Rabinow, *Michel Foucault: Beyond Structuralism and Hermeneutics*, 2nd edn. (Chicago, University of Chicago Press, 1983); while it is insufficiently developed in Simon During, *Foucault and Literature: Towards a Genealogy of Writing* (London, Routledge, 1992). James Bernauer, "Michel Foucault's Ecstatic Thinking," in Bernauer and David Rasmussen, eds, *The Final Foucault* (Cambridge, MA, MIT Press, 1994), hints at bringing Foucault's early work into alignment with his later period, but this relation is, again, underdeveloped.
4. For Foucault's reading of Roussel, see Tilottama Rajan, *Deconstruction and the Remainders of Phenomenology: Sartre, Derrida, Foucault, Baudrillard* (Stanford, CA, Stanford University Press, 2002), pp. 168–198.
5. For Foucault and *Tel Quel*, see Danielle Marx-Scouras, *The Cultural Politics of Tel Quel* (State College, Pennsylvania State University Press, 1996).
6. Michel Foucault, *The Archeaology of Knowledge and the Discourse on Language*, trans. A. M. Sheridan Smith (New York, Pantheon, 1972).
7. For the older account of the historical avant-garde, see Matei Calinescu, *Five Faces of Modernity: Modernism, Avant-Garde, Decadence, Kitsch, Postmodernism* (Durham, NC, Duke University Press, 1987).
8. On "becoming outside," see my genealogical account of the origins of the Language School in terms of the politics of the 1960s: Barrett Watten, "The Turn to Language and the 1960s," *Critical Inquiry* 29.1 (Fall 2002), pp. 139–184.
9. As in Raymond Williams, *The Politics of Modernism: Against the New Conformists* (London, Verso, 1989); see also the critical account of socially "negative" subcultures in Paul Mann, *Masocriticism* (Albany, SUNY Press, 1999).
10. This discussion follows my account of the negativity of the avant-garde in Barrett Watten, *The Constructivist Moment: From Material Text to Cultural Poetics* (Middletown, CT, Wesleyan University Press, 2003), chap. 6.
11. Michel Foucault, *Madness and Civilization: A History of Insanity in the Age of Reason*, trans. Richard Howard (New York, Vintage, 1988), p. 287.
12. In Jacques Derrida's response to Foucault, the aesthetic and social components of madness—that which, precisely, makes it an element of artistic form or social discourse—is bracketed in his account of madness as entailment of subject-centered reason; "Cogito and the History of Madness," in *Writing and Difference*, trans. Alan Bass (Chicago, University of Chicago Press, 1978), pp. 31–63.
13. On Heidegger and art, see Herman Rapaport, *Is There Truth in Art?* (Ithaca, NY, Cornell University Press, 1997).

14. Michel Foucault, "Nietzsche, Genealogy, and History," in *Aesthetics, Method, and Epistemology*, ed. James D. Faubion, *Essential Works of Foucault, 1954–1984*, vol. 2 (New York, The New Press, 1998), pp. 369–92.

15. My work-up of *Moll Flanders* owes everything to Ralph Rader's seminar on the eighteenth-century novel at Berkeley; as Rader liked to say, his position on the descent of the novel in terms of immanently structural criteria was "strong enough to be wrong," and it indeed provided occasions to test the effect of competing examples on his genealogy.

16. Consider the following as a core formulation of the genealogy of the novel, as providing the balance of history and form that *Moll Flanders* lacks: "Richardson's language balances between the claim to historicity and the doctrine of realism, between plot as deception and plot as aesthetic construct, between literary 'acceptance' as an extracted submission to rhetorical force and as a willing suspension of disbelief. And soon its other readers begin to intimate the autonomy and sufficiency of the text, its separability from the reality of which it is the 'authentic' record, by experimenting with generic labels by which it might be designated"—and the novel is born; Michael McKeon, *The Origins of the English Novel, 1600–1740* (Baltimore, The Johns Hopkins University Press, 1987), pp. 361–62.

17. Daniel Defoe, *A General History of Pyrates*, ed. Manuel Schonhorn (New York, Dover, 1999).

18. He might also be interested in the work of Leslie Scalapino, who uses Defoe as a prior model of personal nonidentity in *Defoe* (Los Angeles, Sun and Moon, 1994).

19. Kathy Acker, *I Dreamt I Was a Nymphomaniac: Imagining* (1974/1980), in *Portrait of an Eye* (New York, Grove Press, 1998); Acker, *Pussy, King of the Pirates* (New York, Grove Press, 1996).

20. See Foucault, "Nietzsche, Genealogy, and History." The playful, dissociative element of genealogy, it need be said, is seldom pursued within historical accounts within the tradition of his American reception; for a fine example of genealogical play in avant-garde poetics, see Ben Friedlander, "A Short History of Language Poetry," in *Simulcast: Four Experiments in Criticism* (Tuscaloosa, University of Alabama Press, 2004), pp. 269–308.

21. Michel Foucault, ed., *I, Pierre Rivière, having slaughtered my mother, my sister, and my brother . . . : A Case of Parricide in the 19th Century*, trans. Frank Jellinek (Lincoln, University of Nebraska Press, 1975).

22. Nancy Fraser, "Foucault: A 'Young Conservative'?" in Susan J. Hekman, ed., *Feminist Interpretations of Michel Foucault* (University Park, Pennsylvania State University Press, 1996), pp. 15–38; 34.

23. This privileging the work as scene of decision aligns in some ways with Paul Ricoeur's notion of the narrativity of the self, except that the work may fail or even deny any number of narrative criteria; it may even have the status of a lyric poem, without beginning, middle, or end. One might contrast this sense of form with Ricoeur's: "the gap between the question which engulfs the narrative imagination and the answer of the subject who has been made responsible by the expectation of the other [that is] the secret break at the very heart of commitment. This secret break is what makes the modesty of self-constancy differ from the Stoic pride of rigid self-consistency." One may question how far Acker's immodesty of self-inconsistency is from Ricoeur's narrative, but it is clear how the Stoic alternative to modesty is motivated for Foucault. Paul Ricoeur, *Oneself as Another* (Chicago, University of Chicago Press, 1992), p. 168.

24. Collected as Acker, *Portrait of an Eye*; all pages citations are to this edition.

25. On global recession in the early 1970s, see Ernest Mandel, *The Second Slump: A Marxist Analysis of Recession in the Seventies*, trans. Jon Rothschild (London, NLB, 1978).

26. Material taken from online sources: "The Symbionese Liberation Army," available at http://www.courttv.com/trials/soliah/slahistory_ctv.html; "Symbionese Liberation Army," available at http://www.wikipedia.org/wiki/Symbionese_Liberation_Army.

27. "Seven Years of Crazy Love Music From the Center for Contemporary Music, 1969–1976," available at *http://www.o-art.org/history/70's/CcmCrowd70s/SevenYears/7YearsTape1.html*.
28. Jean-Paul Sartre, *Being and Nothingness*, trans. Hazel E. Barnes (Secaucus, NJ, Citadel Press, 1956), pp. 83–146.
29. Ricoeur, *Oneself as Another*, p. 123; on the dissociation of narrator and character, see the fine dissertation by Susan Beckwith, "Fractured Voices, Failing Bodies: Being and Narrative from the Victorians to Today" (Wayne State University, 2004).
30. Didier Eribon, *Michel Foucault*, trans. Betsy Wing (Cambridge, MA, Harvard University Press, 1991).
31. For my own recent thinking on the moment of liberation, see Watten, "Turn to Language."
32. "CNN Larry King Live: Interview with Patty Hearst," available at http://www.cnn.com/TRANSCRIPTS/0201/22/lkl.00.html.

Devil Father Mine

Laurence A. Rickels

> Rickels does not seem to hold cinema in much esteem. He never considers it
> filmically and appears to approach it as so much mediocre literature.
>
> Review of *The Vampire Lectures* in *Offscreen* 2004

Just Us Girls

In *My Mother: Demonology*, Kathy Acker digs writing in the throwaway defense
mechanisms of the "male language," the language of "the patriarchy." Within a
dizzying relay or rebound of exclusions and implications we can yet discern a line-
up of parallel universals. The first President Bush enters the writing-self's dream
to report the words of his sister: "There are only dreams. This is the *nothing* which
you men call *death*: therefore, in your male language, death and women are friends"
(195). There is, then, another language to which translation or encryptment refers
us. It is a language of memory—the translations or reformulations of the male
language are essentially repressions or forgettings—in which "rhyme" (as the
motor of contaminated and containing slang, jargon, slogans, or word play)
doubles as "the mirror of history" (220). "Thus it became clear that puns, bad
language, and memory are closely conjoined" (187). In *My Mother: Demonology*, as in
Daniel Paul Schreber's *Memoirs of My Nervous Illness*, this bad language is dead-
icated—and it's where the girls are. "According to history, any school of all girls is a
school of the dead" (77). The writing Acker summons demonologically must be
reclaimed from projection. The secondariness or reactivity of projection in the
wake or place of first contact (which subsumes reading, too, conceived as
seconding of the motion of inscription) turns around in this process into new

writing—original screen text—along lines long associated with the Devil. "I have sold myself to the Devil! As do those who write" (129).

The Devil's Lantern

In his *Lucifer Rising* Gavin Baddeley establishes cinema as the "Devil's lantern" (87). The Devil may be the prince of all the occult figures out there, but all the other creatures of the night—of nothingness—always seemed a better generic fit with the film medium. Consider, for example, the cut-and-suture recycling of pre-existing corpus parts comprising Frankenstein's monster—or, for that matter (or mother), Shelley's novel. The vampire, too, since constitutively mirror-image-less and therefore sheer image—the quintessential *Doppelgänger*—can be seen as rising up between the lines of literature in anticipation of cinema. Even when a film like Murnau's *Nosferatu* denies the undead full representation in its own mirror medium, the "phantom" is just the same represented *as* unrepresentable via special-effects stop-starting the motion picture and showing-off manipulation of the print back in the lab. Thus by getting in touch with itself as artificial lab-spawned medium, cinema admits the vampire as its definition or limit concept.

Monster analogies with the movies parallel Freud's insertion of projection into the setting of mourning or unmourning. Untenable wishes re-crossing the mind of the survivor cannot be admitted in close up but only in the long shot of projecting them upon the deceased who, reanimated by the mean-spirited thoughts, ex-presses and acts on a hostility which, in its one-sided, one-way trajectory, gets the survivor around the original messy ambivalence to which the undead creature owes its new release on life and upon the living. The Devil also emerges in the gaps and overlaps between psychic and cinematic projections—but not in the service of finding and keeping in place of losing and weeping. The Devil caters to hugely healthy non-neurotics or—same difference?—psychopaths, subjects, in any event, markedly devoid of inhibitions and precisely not grief-stuck on losses. The Devil's clients are able to substitute for what's missing without complication—to the point that the loss is affirmed in exchange for a new invulnerability or certainty that is the Devil's best offer. Thus the Devil never advertises immortality as the "free gift" you get for joining, but only as finite quality time, time uninterrupted, uncompromised by the uncontrollability of mortality until the set deadline arrives on schedule, the line in time along which you sign when you sign up with the Devil. The Devil does not indwell the projection of the other (undead or live). The Devil's clients contemplate instead the projection out of nothing of a world of their own making. What lies between, however, the Devil's inevitable medium in the egos of innocent bystanders, is his projective typecasting as laughable trickster. At the same time, as Freud observes of the doodling caricatures on the margins of the superego's dictation, the butt of all jokes is the child's early–easy identification with the father, the child taking it up the wisecrack.

While the Devil has no use for vampire-lovers, God-worshippers, suicides or any of the other immortality neurotics, it amuses him to watch your average inhibited imagination victimized by its projections. Anton LaVey, presumably in his day Satan's representative, recapped the projections that rebound to the gory imagination of parental guidance:

> Your Apocalypse is here . . . Credit me for the revolution, but credit yourselves for the forms that it has taken . . . Whenever I got on TV or the radio, I was given a few seconds to say what they desperately needed me for . . . If Satanism was so hot, why wasn't I able to talk about it? . . . A "Satanic survivor" could grunt out 15 belabored minutes of applauded testimony, while a real Satanist was lucky to be heard above two whole minutes of studio idiots gasping and jeering. Now, in your End Times, you blame Death Metal and its influence on youth . . . YOU listened to the warnings and examples set forth by the Blattys, Pazders, Geraldos, Oprahs . . . and their identity-starved stooges . . . YOU provided media saturation informing them what "real" Satanists do, what kind of noises they make when possessed. YOU encouraged them to rebel by the aesthetic standards YOU provided . . . Your hysterical plan has backfired. YOU brought about your own Apocalypse, like the stupid masochistic victims that you are. ("To: All Doomsayers . . . & Assorted Tremblers," 4–7)

LaVey always tried to affirm the projections recycled time and again to represent *and* repress the Devil as sleazy journalist, abject bureaucrat, or used-car salesman (whose favorite verb, as learned from social scientists, is "utilize"). Drawing on his career as circus carney, LaVey affirmed magic pranks, inflatable companions, and all the rest remaindered in the back of pulp magazines. If LaVey admired H. P.

Lovecraft to the point of including the Cthulhu legend in his Black Mass, it is because the author, appearances and apparitions notwithstanding, could be viewed as cultivating, in the reversed mode of disgust, the same tenets as those guiding LaVey's affirmation or exhibitionism of our abjection relations with the Devil. The Devil not only watches but also inspires a neurotic medium of disgust that Lovecraft raised to the power of literature: a body or corpus gets built in slo-mo out of returning blockages or repressions, something any body might attend to while coming down off the ecstatic cling of certain drug-induced de-repressions. The dread mongrelization that lowers the doom in Lovecraft's "The Call of Cthulhu" lingers, malingers in the extended span of time right before and during the saving repression. Lovecraft does not make the jumpcut to one more projection for the rote recognition of inhibited minds. LaVey, for his part or party, stays with the scandal in a megalo-political mode. In "A Plan," for instance, he bases his forecast of a victory of Satanism over Christianity on the melting plot whereby a new majority of half Jews and other hybrids (coming soon) will turn to the pedigree and look of evil "rooted in Judeo/Nazism" (20). These children of mixed unions—following the lead of the half Jews—will deal with the "and" that was dealt them "through new common denominators that render established stigmas as inconsequential" (21).

Hereditary Jewish culture is a perfect springboard for anti-Christian senti-ment. The Jews have a foot in the door as the only historically consistent scapegoated enemies of Christ . . . To be a Satanist is, by association, already to be aligned with the universal devil Jew. The Jews have always had the Devil's name. They just haven't owned up to or taken pride in it, but rather have attempted to defend themselves against it. Instead of declaring that Jesus was a nut and a shit disturber and he got what he deserved and we'd do it all over again, they decided to infiltrate the Christian world and survive that way . . . Just as the Nazis "Aryanized" certain needed Jews, we will see even more of the same phenomenon, given the pragmatically Jewish/Satanic connection. Gentiles without a drop of Jewish blood might concoct genea-logical evidence of a Jewish great-grandfather, thus making them by heredity, generational Satanists . . . The only place a rational amalgam of proud, admitted, Zionist Odinist Bolshevik Nazi Imperialist Socialist Fascism will be found—and championed—will be in the Church of Satan. (21–22)

LaVey's link to projection seems here creatively or therapeutically interventionist. To get to this point, however, LaVey deliberately inhabits and passes through a crossfire of the projections that accrue to the Devil as his medium.

Screen Text

A 2004 remake of an old idea—called "Lucid Dreaming"—extolled the benefits of controlling your dream world to the point that one might even summon the body double of a desired object for dreamy sexual contact. At this point we get reacquainted with the notion of the succubus (or incubus) as the demonic occasion for turbulent dreaming. In J. K. Huysmans's *La-Bas* and *En Route*, the Satanist Madame Chantelouve exercises this sexual power over the dream thoughts of the protagonist. While writing *My Mother: Demonology*, Kathy Acker dreamed up new writing sources and reserves. She trained herself to control her dreaming, to pick up a dream right where she left off when she last awakened, and to remember her dreams intact and undisclosed. She was not, however, interested in the other world of dreaming. Or, as the writing-self advises in *My Mother: Demonology*, "I have always despised fantasy" (225). Acker placed her body and corpus on one continuum with as many projections as she could throw a fit with. Dreaming relies on projection, as does the delusional system of the psycho, his and her new world or word order. (Freud once noted in passing that even the ego, bottom line, is a projection of the body.) For long hauls in the composition of her demonology, Acker watched movies and metabolized them, first in her sleeping, dreaming state, then in writing. At the same time she sought to extract writing from her sexualized body, a body massively traversed by projections, including the cinematic ones to which the body skewered on a dildo was also responding before or after or during its dream response. While thus laying claim to new frontier zones of writing, Acker was also seeking, as the writing-self declares in *My Mother: Demonology*, "the power to reclaim myself" (249).

For her demonological exploration of projection Acker ostensibly departed from her signature work of incorporation of novels with recognition value whereby even the pre-curse of originality could be lifted. In *My Mother: Demonology* even *Wuthering Heights* is in the first place a movie (146) before it passes through the dreaming, remembering, writing, reading body into demonology. The mother part of the novel's title also emerges in this series (on the other side of the "colon"): "Then I dreamed or saw a movie . . . There was a woman holding a huge dog by a leash. She had no eyes. It was my mother. She said, 'I've been looking for you.' I woke up. As I woke up, I realized that my mother was trying to murder me through me" (251).

In "Reading the Lack of the Body: The Writing of the Marquis de Sade," Acker identifies rejection of the mother as the trait distinguishing certain female characters—at least in de Sade's "patriarchy" from "hell"—as enjoying a "propensity for freedom" (67): "The daughter who does not reject her mother interiorizes prison" (69). Acker underscores that in Eugénie's formulation of her matricidal wish lies above all certainty: "in *Philosophy In the Bedroom*, Eugénie, no longer a virgin in a number of ways, admits to her female teacher that the most 'certain impulse' in her heart, note that she does not say 'deepest,' is to kill her mother" (68). Certainty rather than passion gets the mother—the off-limits body, the missing body, the loss that one cannot lose—out of the way so the daughter (or, interchangeably, the son) can make backend deals with the primal father (or Devil father). Dolmancé's counsel tries to make of the interchangeability of gender in this primal phase a masculinist virtue or privilege: "Women can 'transform . . . themselves into men by choosing to engage in sodomy'" (69). But "to have the breach open always" applies equally to mother, little boy, and little girl at the same time that the third-party intruder, before the advent of Oedipus and substitution, monopolizes sexual difference as his exclusive right to penetrate. This is the era of the anal theory of birth. That's why the woman's reproductive body, conceived as article of faith, has no hold or place here. The privileging of sodomy therefore requires, in the outside chance that the wrong orifice is penetrated in the polymorphous activity of orgies, a woman's right to abortion. As Acker observes: "Only a belief in God, rather than in Nature, could lead a human to value an embryo more than herself " (70).

In league with the Devil, the writing-self in *My Mother: Demonology* can address something dead, something of her own, as the world and in the word of death: "Since my childhood is dead, in speaking of it I shall be speaking of something dead, but I shall do so in order to speak of the world of death, of the Kingdom of Darkness, or of Transparency" (185). The Devil gets the writing-self across or through or beyond—trans—the parents, with the mother at the front of the line. The mother, a suicide, is doubly inside the writing-self trying to take her out. "That night I dreamed my last dream. In which my mother tried to kill me. She didn't succeed. Then someone else tried to murder me. When I asked who the murderer might be, the Voice told me that it wasn't my mother. It was a question of time. 'But it must be my mother,' I replied. 'Yes: it's your mother who's now inside you'" (226). To get herself out from under the dead wait with mother, and transform the murderous merger into writing—"When I was five years old, I knew that Mother wanted me to be a red or dead child" (52)— the writing-self passes through p-unitive relations with the pre-Oedipal father, the Devil father. This father—in whom she recognizes that the quality of evil inheres in the quality of artistry (101)—dutifully sets out to abuse his daughter in order to realize his ultimate work of art, a masterpiece of horror:

"In order to see horror, I have to touch or fuck horror." (99)

Father said, "To paint horror, I must violate both vision and my own child." (100)

"I must see horror. I said that to see must be to touch or become what is seen." (103)

The writing-self was all along telling "everything" in order that the Devil father would "kill" her "faster" (24). Or, since murder and dream are interchangeable (via the lack viewed as central to both [35]), the Devil father should dream her faster, hold her fast in the dream body, bind her in projection, meet the exhaustion of "everything" said and done with the exhaustion, wasting, of the body and its projective sensurround. "I always want to test everything to the point of death. Beyond" (24). But death metamorphoses or translates—back and forth—into dream, into projection.

Red is the color of dreams, of horror, of murder, of writing. Just as "led" follows or serves the guiding verb "to lead," so "red," for "read," could give us the clear text and past tense of reading, which, as Acker underscores, is already also writing. "The more that I write my novels, the more it seems to me that to write is to read" ("Reading the Lack," 66). In the beginning was the red word, the word as deed of writing. The pact with the Devil father soon follows. But in both Goethe's *Faust* and *My Mother: Demonology*, the pact goes into effect only with the assistance of the witch. In order to enter "the library of the witch" "where there was red somewhere" (125), the writing-self drags the paternal deed of her soul's possession down into the maternal body and underworld of writing/reading/remembering. "My mother spoke: From now on, whenever I dreamed, I called it *going back to the* witch" (116). "And so I began descending, *as in my dreams*, walking down the spiral staircase that led to the witch's library" (261).

In her study of Goethe's *Faust* as transference prop that in the course of Freud's self-analysis allowed him to articulate and re-experience various relations with the Devil father, Sabine Prokhoris takes both Freud and Goethe at their word when Faust's rejuvenation as promised by Mephistopheles cannot proceed without the assistance of the witch. In Freud's summons, the witch is also named metapsychology, the ultimate articulation of those otherwise discarded self-analytic spookulations to which psychoanalysis owes its inscription and application. According to Prokhoris, every paternal function in this Faustian–Freudian discourse "is gradually transmuted into unsettling, uncontrollable maternal terrain, subject as it eventually is to the witch. What one may call 'self-analysis' is this very transformation" (74).

Goethe's *Faust* serves as station identification for transferences passing through or into Freud's self-analysis. But it is also a cite-specific medium mediated by the transference it mediates. Prokhoris reads Goethe's lines of dead-ication (to the reunion with spirits for which his completed *Faust* stands) within the grid of associations and contexts wherein Freud compulsively summons them, in letter and in spirits.

> This commerce with spirits and . . . this love act consummated with them, this fort–da, governs the self analysis. It is abundantly represented in Freud's dreams. And it likewise marks off the space of every analysis. That is, it clears a broad path for the transference, to cite Freud's own words, or rather Goethe's, whom Freud quotes in rather surprising fashion, leaving the impression that an irresistible force has compelled him to reproduce the poet's words—as if they had materialized from somewhere else, like the shades they speak of. This same commerce with the spirit world is in evidence . . . in the upsurge of ideas leading toward metapsychology . . . For metapsychology is the theoretical expression of this transference; it is what brings it to light. (89)

Her focus on the supplementary turn to the witch—and to the witch metapsychology—gives Prokhoris license and motivation to lump together vampiric spirits of the departed with the Devil. But otherwise the recycled blood of undead suckers is not the spot of blood you're in when you sign the pact with the Devil. The Devil's blood spots are fecal, menstrual, a medium for signing and all the other smear tactics of certainty, Dad certainty. But then the spot of blood is out, out of this limited economy once mixed into the witch's brew, the resource for red writing. If the pre-Oedipal father as Devil must turn to the pre-Oedipal mother as witch (who is there to serve him but with powers all her own), then it is in order to give the missing body a rest or breast, the prize of doubled life that the Devil promises in his backend deals. In turn, the only father who can be resurrected is the early father joined at this rip-and-tear line with the pre-Oedipal mother. Thus, Prokhoris argues, the ambiguous Devil in the case of "demonological possession" Freud analyzes is "the father . . . truly brought back to life:"

> He cannot exist in this diabolical form, in which he is again endowed with the attributes and features of the primal father, until the venerated, adored, deified father has disappeared . . . Only when this exaltation comes to an end is the diabolical father, who had been imprisoned by the majesty of the paternal function, at last set free. (117)

As becomes apparent—a parent—on the Devil's body in Freud's case study, "the attributes and features of the primal father" are those that must be shared with or re-turned to the pre-Oedipal mother. The part or parting objects to which the father owes his projection (notably penetrating penis and buttocks) must double the breast tumescent with milk. This realignment is the objective relation of Satanic orgiastic sexuality. It is also the significance the built body shares sexually with the fuck-dolly.

The writing-self in *My Mother: Demonology* passes from imprisonment by the mother's missing body to the sexuality the Devil father first administers.

> I was imprisoned by my mother and had no father. My body was all I had. (10)
>
> I escaped my mother because sexuality was stronger than her . . . The acceptance of this separation between sexuality and being was an invention of hell. (14)

At the same time the writing-self heeds a "lesson" in "translation" that, like the Goethe in Freud, is citational introject: "Hear the breasts' voices" (32).

Rear-View Mirrors

Published in 1922, Lou Andreas-Salomé's *The Devil and His Grandmother* is submitted by Luisa de Urtubey (in her study *Freud and the Devil*), together with other Devil interpretations by Freud's disciples (including Otto Pfister, Otto Rank, and Theodor Reik) which appeared at that same time, as proof that there were indeed blanks to be filled when Freud foreclosed the Devil in his analysis of Daniel Paul Schreber's *Memoirs of My Nervous Illness*—or rather, in other words, when the Devil foreclosed on Freud. De Urtubey cooks up the Schreber case with close attention to the details. Schreber's family saw to it that most of the psycho's recollection of his soul murder was excised from the memoirs. But Schreber's passing reference to soul murder's similarity to Faust's pact with the Devil was left alone as was his historical note regarding some of his own ancestors who sought to extend their life-spans through such pacts of soul murder. De Urtubey notes that as Schreber goes on with his listing of ancestral soul murders and (since his persecutor's influence over Schreber extends through both families' histories) the consequent transformation of certain of Dr Flechsig's ancestors into "Auxiliary Devils," Schreber uses the phrase, "appetite comes with eating." Thus the relationship of soul murder, a pact with the Devil father through which an increase in life can be obtained at, say, Schreber's expense, is, de Urtubey concludes, a regressed representation of castration as cannibalism and as such a most extreme expression of one of the forms of the phantasm of seduction by the father (79–81).

Andreas-Salomé introduces us into the cycle of the deceased's digestion under the Devil's guidance. The Devil proposes marriage to a newly dead girl crawling out of her grave's decomposition to find herself alive again, alive to the prospects of hell (4–7). In hell her gravesite is rear-side seating up against the ass of the Devil's grandmother. In contrast, God admits souls only after they have been "de-assed" (7). At bottom, the dead in hell are free to be themselves, to create or re-create themselves interminably. "Satanized you enjoy yourselves for the first time completely: Give yourself to me—and you have been given to yourself " (7). The love the Devil offers his bride-would-be is "selfless" as only "Devil's love" can be: "I am nothing but the space in which you burn bright, nothing but the emptiness in which you fulfill yourselves . . . With my border of many thousand sparks, I proceed as illumination in order to celebrate you" (10).

The Devil's proposal is knocked out by an accidental reversal in grandmother's anal productivity: an undigested living baby falls by the rear side into the lap of the girl's untenable affirmation of reproductive life. What follows is all the show the Devil must rally against reproductive creativity: the girl's body gets laid out as waste production in the projective lab space of anal birth or animation.

The Devil summons an audience of prospective clients to view his own brand of motion picture. The good citizens agree to grant the Devil a captive audience.

> "Well then: that business is done. Let's go then! For my little dolly has likely done her business, too, in the golden pot" (Rapidly increasing darkness in which one can only vaguely make out the high smooth wall pushing up in place of the abyss . . . The wall surface illuminates itself; in rapid sequence animated pictures glide across. Music starts to play) "Did I catch a disappointed cry: 'Just a movie'?" (27)

But no, this is the film from hell: in it the viewers will see accomplished "what was not yet in" them, namely the "grinning decomposition" of their "basic life force" (28). To this end, the Devil himself will play an original role in this film, "not as image of something that has happened, no: as a living embodied happening in the film:" "Everything there passes by as depiction; only I, myself mirror-image and illusion, am only there my essential self " (30).

The silent film wraps nature views around the audience. Suddenly the meadow scene pulls apart revealing "a hole in the film, brightly illuminated, as happens with used-up reels" (32). Next the film steps back from representation into the background of rapidly alternating scenes; in the foreground the runaway bride crashes through the projections with the Devil in pursuit. She drops onto a bed—"the film bed." The Devil proceeds to undress her: "This makes for a show in its own right in that the film brings each body part before the eyes of the audience in penetrating enlargement" (32). Next the bride makes the cut, the Devil's cut or portion. The Devil cuts her up along the dotted lines of her strip show's fragmenting projection:

> Now he pulls his tail out from behind his coat tails, grabs its end between bunches of hair and sharpens it with his pocket knife, whereupon it begins to glow red. Then he plunges it into the navel of the sleeping girl; from there he

draws his cuts in star formation. Then, in similar fashion, he cuts around each of the nipples; then around the mouth; finally he slices up arms and legs. (33)

But when snuff is enough the result is abstract creation, which only but especially in its cleanliness betrays the extreme anality it wipes clean. "What balm for the eyes— without blood and wounds! How clean and exact the specimen! As a wonderful mosaic of death and life, uncorrupted in forms and in colors" (33). A puzzle play with mosaic pieces—affirmed as the Devil's speciality in the area of creation—picks up where the bride's body and the consummating cutting left off. "What you call decay and dismemberment becomes for me in the first place plaything" (35).

The Devil organizes the pieces into patterns of his own invention. But he also piles up "spook formations." The combination prospects are endless, unlike all "works" that, like the life forms themselves, must pass on, fall apart, "decay like spooks." The mixed metaphorizing with "spooks" gives the lie or slip to the Devil's abstract game. Thus when the film medium projects the pieces of the bride larger than life, their images unfold "as though sharply animated by the drive to exist." What we see here we also recognize: her lidless eyeballs "out of which spectacularly clear despair without hope looks at you—grief over that which is irretrievably dead" (34). Hence, in lieu of the mourning that strikes up between the scrubbed-down lines of cutting—a place his grandmother or mother will fulfill for him—the Devil commits suicide, which his mourners prefer to view as his becoming whole again in re-union with God. The pull of this promised union, however, doesn't hold a candle to the push of suicidal grief accumulated in unmourning and undeath.

According to his grandmother, the Devil is by now beside the pointlessness of his supernatural existence. His mission came full circle, completed itself, with Christ's mission accomplished: the Devil deified man and then Christ humanized God (44). The Devil therefore exposes himself to direct light and vaporizes like film stock. Now that the walking sheer image is gone, the primacy of the image can be hitched to the ascendancy of belief. No image without belief in it: hence the image that everything ultimately is equals image of belief. Death, too, is but an image, a reflection of (belief in) resurrection (54–55). But in closing, one of the girls wishes that the Devil's rebirth or comeback be her vehicle. What drove the Devil to suicide will pull him back: the return trajectory along which the dead clog, interrupt, and break up the transmission of union or unity.

Rhyme-Word Death

Composed in Goethean good measure—along the assembly lines comprising the portable *Faust*, lines Goethe gave (according to Karl Kraus) for easy recall and recitation—*The Devil and His Grandmother* is on one continuum with an otherwise surprising partner in rhyme: the Devil's doggerel in Michelle Smith and Lawrence Pazder's *Michelle Remembers*. For better or verses, the Devil's rhymes only *seem* banal—they *are* evil, as, we are assured, only intelligent life can be. Father Guy is consulted by Dr Pazder and his patient, Michelle: "If you look up Satan in a theological dictionary, it will say that he is known to speak in rhymes. And the form of the rhymes reveals his personality. They do not have an orderly structure, but they are very intelligent. And very deceptive. They all have meaning . . . Satan will not humiliate himself to speak like ordinary people" (209).

The encrypted lines directed both over our heads and smack dab in the middlebrow are also the audio portion of the Devil's hands-on performance of violent cutting. While reciting his Master Plan, the Devil whittles away at the sculpted wooden body of the crucified Christ.

> During the course of the ceremony, he would whittle away at the carved statue . . . until nothing was left. Symbolically of the way he works in the world—undercutting—he would start his whittling at the foot of the cross and proceed upward.
>
> > First cut away the feet;
> > Make a man feel incomplete.
> > Lose his footing, lose his ground;
> > Lose the way to walk around.
> > . . .
>
> He had reached the loins of the corpus.
> > Then I chip away at the part
> > They say should be connected to the heart.
> > But I can separate it with one cut,
> > And make it separate, make it smut. (227–228)

When the chips are all off the old block—leaving nothingness and the prospect of the ritual's endless repetition—the Devil's ability "to project colossal three-dimensional images illustrating what he was saying" (223) takes over: "The sinister illusion was now a bottomless hole within a raging fire. Falling into the hole . . . were houses, cars, books, numbers, paintings, animals, coffins—the whole world seemed to be tumbling into the pit" (230).

But the bottom line of projected nothingness is the bodily cut. The Devil sees to it that we—who should go forth and multiply—are all cut up over his slicing of life:

> Seizing the knife, the Beast drove it into the girl's chest. With a few violent strokes he cut out the heart and, scooping it up, he heaved it into the fire.
>> Twelve times two, and then add four.
>> Cut it in half and then there's more.
> With another strong stroke he cut the body in half . . . Working harder now with the knife, he cut the halves in half, then cut the segments in pieces. (217–218)

The cutting climbs over multiples to grow the body up and away into projected parts.

A cut not on the screen, but secreted away, exceeds the wounds on projective display, to which it nevertheless belongs. A ritual mutilation marking the members of the Devil's inner circle is the last secret Michelle lets go in therapy at or as the end of her total recall of the projected Vision of Hell:

> "You see Hell!" . . . And as he spoke, the walls of the round room faded away, and it seemed to the child that she was in the middle of an enormous movie, with gigantic, soaring images . . . Below them, as if in some ultimate nightmare, Michelle could see masses of starving people, bodies on battle-fields, a million acts of cruelty somehow made visual all at once.
>> There's people with arms that are bleeding . . . There's people with no eyes, and they're bleeding from their eyes. There's people that's got no noses! And there's people that got ears cut off . . . An-n-n-n . . . and there's people with missing fing . . . (213)

So there's one body part in the series that she can't part with—except by performing its cutting off. The girl just can't divulge it. But Dr Pazder won't budge. She must tell if she wants to get well. She gives him the finger that makes the cut that gives the secret handshake: "It's always the middle finger . . ." She looked at Dr Pazder in terror. "Oh, God, I said too much. Am I going to die?" (215). The fuck finger goes down in the transference where it is left unanalyzed, uncut, and wholly at the service of holy healing. Now give me your hand! During Michelle's trial or test, symbols of the Christian faith—with Ma Mere at the front of the line—hover above in love during Michelle's trial while installing the repressed memory of her sojourn with Satan with a time release set to reveal all once a match can be made with ears to hear. They leave behind a placeholder, even a pronoun, through which the psychiatrist enters Michelle's life. Outside the book's ending Dr Pazder takes Michelle to be his wife. The Pazders bypass the witch. "For it is the witch who makes it possible for the words which initiate the cure to become analytic, which is to say, transferential, discourse" (Prokhoris, 91).

The Devil's projective medium is subtended by the whirring network of recording devices whereby the in-session dynamic is doubled and erased as record speaking for itself. "Once the explanations were arrived at, sometime later, it all was fairly intelligible—almost impossible to conceive of, to hold in the mind, but at least intelligible. But while Michelle was reliving it—bringing it up from her depths and pouring it out for Dr. Pazder while the video camera hummed, recording her gestures and expressions—it was confusing in the extreme" (214). This admission of the setting of revelations in place of transference introduces the one memory—the missing middle finger—"that Michelle could not bring herself to divulge."

LaVey's impatient exclamation in fact precisely addresses this live repression of memory: "Where was Freudian wisdom when psychiatry like *Michelle Remembers* was validated by the media?" ("To: All Doomsayers . . . & Assorted Tremblers," 6). I, too, remember the 1980s, when our mass mediatization ran on the child-abuse charge. One Devilish phase of the transference that Sándor Ferenczi identified in 1913 was the phase everyone was going through in the 1980s. Freud and the Satanists were codependants in cross-examination for the seduction offence.

Mine

Among the parting shots of *My Mother: Demonology*, we find a cut above the rest, a cut in life that, just like bad language and puns, follows the beat of memory. "It's necessary to cut life into bits, for neither the butcher store nor the bed of a woman who's giving birth is as bloody as this. Absurdity, blessed insolence that saves, and connivance are found in these cuts, the cuts into 'veracity.' . . . All these are found in the cuts . . . The entire human being is found there" (267). Dario Argento's horror film *Suspiria*, one of the sustaining introjects of *My Mother: Demonology*, follows out the cutting across vision that admits demonization or projection.

One girl arrives at an all red school only to witness another girl running. (Which school? The one where all the teachers, all of them, are witches.) We're on the outside looking in on the runaway in the bathroom. But then we're inside there with her, too. She looks out into darkness and sees herself mirrored in the pane. But then: two cat's eyes. Hirsute creaturely arms stab her without letting up, without letting go. At the end of the laundry line, her rebound breaks the glass ceiling below and splits the second victim whose face is divided up by sharp shards. No eye witnesses. The only outsider working at the school is a blind man walking. In time the seeing-eye dog chews out his throat. The catch to this movie, like a catch in the throat, is that the secret word the new girl overheard dead girl running cry out—"irises"—not only marks, as flower password, the secret spot of extended lifetime the witches are in every night with their centuries-old coven mistress, but also names the filmy surface of eyesight the film slices or otherwise secretes away in order to see better.

The iris, in German, is the rainbow of the eye. As the female Devil in love with the book dealer protagonist intones (in *The Club Dumas*, another novel that can barely contain between its lines the projection momentum that will get it into pictures): "The rainbow is the bridge between heaven and earth. It will shatter at the end of the world, once the Devil has crossed it on horseback" (204).

At one turning point in Arturo Pérez-Reverte's *The Club Dumas*, the protagonist Corso deals with a collector who must periodically sell a volume to maintain the rest. Once another sacrifice has been made the collector goes back to playing his violin "to summon the ghosts of his lost books" (165). When Corso first makes his acquaintance, the collector is doubled over with the burden of choosing between two of his favorite collectibles, the best of the rest, a Virgil edition, featuring illustrations of Aeneas in hell, and a first-edition copy of *De re metallica* by Georgius Agricola. The bottom lines of the Devil's projective medium are suspended here: between hell and mining.

The novel drops these lines within a relay of self-reflections aggrandized through inter-reference to address all of letters—and their spirits. And yet the titular plot, which proves diversionary, not even a subplot of the Devil fiction, is the haunted text. But then even the main text devoted to the Devil—as the author or subject of Black Magic volumes that contribute not to melancholy self-collection but instead serve a certain purpose that uses them up—is subsumed at the end by a twist-off of literature's self-involvement as medium down to the fine printing. Two printers specializing in restoration of collectible ancient books were commissioned to restore without acknowledgement—in other words, to counterfeit—one of the original illustrations in the Black Magic book signed by the Devil. Only the collector who uses the pages to undergo the magical transformation or crossover knows for sure: we only see the man die in what looks like a botched attempt.

Roman Polanski swerves away from the book's title, the haunted plot from which it hangs, and all the reflexive loops beyond and in between, and focuses instead on the titles of his film *The Ninth Gate*. The film's opening titles and first scene open the surface wide to admit light that ultimately takes a double shining to the end, the convergence of the illuminated, illustrated book plates as of the film's titles with the binding brightness of Corso's transforming sexual union with the Devil. But all this depth or diversification never leaves the span of a projector's illumination, the surface of the filmic image.

David Seltzer wrote the novel *The Omen* after the film was already folding out of his original screenplay. As novel that one could not but write or read as basis for the film version, as artefact in the older medium handing its sentence down on the reductive newer medium to which it sells out, through which it seeks new lease on shelf life, *The Omen* is of necessity in the post-production line of metabolizing and reclaiming projections. The movie *The Omen* included a medium-specific side effect or symptom of the Devil's occult mediation. A press photographer's shots of future victims already showed the "light writing" on the wall: the forecast of the future event was outlined in light smears or scratches that looked like flaws in the photographic process. The screen version recalls spiritist photography in which ghostly presences invisible to the living participants in a seance were just the same recorded through the camera's eye. According to Freud, the death wish we cannot bear to acknowledge as our own when a living target joins the ranks of the departed dictates that what we see is what we forget. We always only have a ghost of a chance of making the connection at the mediatized remove and reversal brought to us by haunting. In the case of the photographs inside the film *The Omen*, we witness the advance preview of the fateful fulfillment of the Devil's omnipotent wish is his command. The novel can't let the photographic sign or symptom go:

> It was the same sort of defect he'd had a few months ago in the shot of the nanny at the Thorn estate. This time it involved the shots of the priest. Once again it seemed to be a flaw on the emulsion . . . Even more curious, it seemed linked to the subject, the strange blur of movement hanging above the priest's head as though it were somehow actually there . . . Not only did the blemish disappear in the two shots of the Marine, but when it reappeared in the final shot, it was smaller in size, relative to the size of the priest. (63)

The photographer considers recent theories about film emulsion's sensitivity to heat, including that of the residual energy that ghosts can be seen to embody.

> What was the meaning of energy that clung to the outside of a human form? Did it come at random, or did it have some *meaning*? . . . Anxiety was known to create energy, this the principle of the polygraph used for lie detector tests. That energy was electrical in nature. Electricity was also heat. Perhaps the heat generated by extreme anxiety burst through human flesh and could thus be photographed surrounding people in states of great stress. (64)

He tests the theory by photographing patients in a terminal ward who know they are dying, subjects he could presume, therefore, to be in states of extreme stress. Nothing. He redevelops the pictures of priest and nanny: "It was plain, in enlargement, that something was actually there. The naked eye had not seen it, but the nitrate had responded. Indeed, there were invisible images in the air" (64–65). In the novel the photo speculations outnumber their matching on-screen special effects. The novel's parting shot (as seen NOT in the screen version) is staggered via Before and After photography. Out of the reporters' shots photographs are developed in which one can make out the ectoplasmic lowering of the doom on the car taking son-of-Satan to his new and improved home.

Photographs (like dreams) can recognize and forecast what passes before the naked eye unseen. They hold the place of legibility alongside the projections that in Devil fiction must also make the cut and touch the wound.

It seems almost metapsychological fact that Devil fiction requires the loop between literary and screen media. *Rosemary's Baby*, *The Ninth Gate*, *The Exorcist*, *The Sentinel*, *The Possession of Joel Delaney*—all of them, all of them, titles of films based on books. Barring the lineage of or in letters, Devil movies can turn instead to the slasher formula. The self-reflexivity of slasher movies touches the outside wounds of murderous violence that the mass media at large must be seen or watched as (in every sense) containing. In *The Devil and His Grandmother*, screen-deep projections are accompanied by cuts, losses, and screams that are as real as the audience the Devil summons. In Lamberto Bava's *Demons* a demonizing wound is transmitted via an infinite regress of screens within screens. A demon mask hanging in the lobby wounds a member of the audience who tries it on. This cut is simulcast in the film (within the film) as the wounding of one character by a demon mask discovered in a grave, a cut that will transform this person into the first screen demon. But in the meantime the wound on the audience's side of the spectacle demonizes one member, driving her to ravage another one. The demon epidemic on screen meets the epidemic soon raging up and down the aisles when the second demonized movie-goer rips through the screen and becomes everyone else's scream memory.

The *Scream* trilogy recycled and reclaimed this staging of self-reflexivity within the slasher sensurround of violence of everyday life. *Scream* reverses the mythic-historic setting of *Demons*: Nostradamus, the movie inside this movie tells us, predicted Hitler's rise to power and this demon invasion coming at us. But both *Demons* and *Scream* prey and stay together via the Mass of murder.

The loop through the wound is basic to the Devil's hold on projection: yes, it's a self-contained world after all created out of nothing, but all its terms are not generated out of itself, do not come down to nothing. Next to nothing, this world throws at least one loop through the cut that cuts in on the endless fall, its bottom line, the bottom you hit even when you fall into the abyss, into nothingness. Something literal, something projected: that's what Devil fictions are made of.

When Milton reaches across his own blindness to conjure the abyssal fall of the rebel angels and dictate his representation of unrepresentability to his seeing-I daughter, he has the falling angels hit bottom in an underworld that precedes the creation of the world as the bottom line of worldly creation. Out of the burning fecal wasteland, Milton and Lucifer extract the shining ore of mining, our primal technology: palaces of gold can be built—as well as the infernal war machines with which Lucifer arms his soldiers for the second assault upon the heavens. The writing-self in *My Mother: Demonology* conjures her own escape artistry as the abyssal immersion in language that contains itself as her fiction: "I write in the dizziness that seizes that which is fed up with language and attempts to escape through it: the abyss named *fiction*" (80). Call it the fiction in the abyss or the transference in the transmission of knowledge—it is what Acker saw red writing.

The Marquis de Sade, a Devil father in Acker's reading, seeks to seduce "us, his readers, into the labyrinth where nothing matters because, there, nothing can matter" ("Reading the Lack of the Body," 71). And again: "Every labyrinth is a machine whose purpose is to unveil chaos" (73). But peeling the veil from chaos or nothingness can also resonate as pealing it: letting it ring out and up from the bottom of your art. There is a labyrinth of bottom lines that does not fit a finite/infinite machine or logic. Acker—like Freud, like Goethe—supplements the pact psychology of Satanic doubling and nothingness with the turn to and trope of the witch. On his own the Devil father cannot grant a new beginning but can only defer the end for the finite time it takes for it to arrive after all. Turning to the witch named fiction, extending through her offices the range of the Devil's best offer, Acker takes the plunge through language, catching fire from the projections around and passing through her, until, hitting bottom lines of red writing, she begins again from scratch (from Old Scratch).

Works Cited

Acker, Kathy, *My Mother: Demonology* (New York, Pantheon Books, 1993).
———— "Reading the Lack of the Body: The Writing of the Marquis de Sade," in Kathy Acker, *Bodies of Work* (London, Serpent's Tail, 1997), pp. 66–80.
Andreas-Salomé, Lou, *Der Teufel und seine Grossmutter* (Jena, Eugen Diederichs, 1922).

Baddeley, Gavin, *Lucifer Rising* (London, Plexus, 1999).

LaVey, Anton Szandor, "A Plan." *Satan Speaks!* (Los Angeles, Feral House, 1998), pp. 20–22.

_____ "To: All Doomsayers, Head-Shakers, Hand-Wringers, Worrywarts, Satanophobes, Identititty Christers, Survivor Counselors, Academia Nuts, & Assorted Tremblers," *Satan Speaks!*, pp. 4–7.

Pérez-Reverte, Arturo, *The Club Dumas*, trans. Sonia Soto (New York, Vintage International, 1998 [1993]).

Prokhoris, Sabine, *The Witch's Kitchen. Freud, "Faust", and the Transference*, trans. G. M. Goshgarian (Ithaca, Cornell University Press, 1995 [1988]).

Seltzer, David, *The Omen* (New York, Signet Books, 1976).

Smith, Michelle, and Pazder, Lawrence, *Michelle Remembers* (New York, Congdon & Lattès inc., 1980).

Urtubey, Luisa de, *Freud et le diable* (Paris, Presses Universitaires de France, 1983).

Kathy Acker:
"Because I Want to Live Forever in Wonder"

Nayland Blake

1. Dates

I'm listening to the X-Ray Spex single "Oh Bondage Up Yours" backed with "I'm a Cliché," a record made in 1977. It's one of the precious pieces of vinyl I bought at Bleecker Bob's, the first store in New York to stock punk records, both imported and homegrown. At the time, buying singles was a crap shoot: you knew nothing about the bands since most of them had barely been together long enough to make a record. Every week there were a dozen singles by bands you'd never heard of. You picked out the ones with the best covers, the most shocking names, the colored vinyl; and for every ten you bought eight were good and of those eight, four would be incredible, a few felt life-altering.

"Oh Bondage . . ." starts like this: an adolescent, slightly congested voice comes out of an echoing void. "Some people think little girls should be seen and not heard, but I think OH BONDAGE UP YOURS ONE TWO THREE FOUR!!" On the final word, a sloppy drum roll and the band has already started, too fast and crashing into each other: guitar, bass, and drums at once, topped by a bleating saxophone that's playing something that's not melody exactly and isn't a riff either, mostly two notes alternating like a siren. Buoyed by the band, the singer (Poly Styrene, born Marion Elliot, who was nineteen when this was recorded) starts bellowing about being tied up, being a victim, being a "slave to you all." She's a teenaged, mixed-race girl and her voice is shouting desire and disgust, she's squawking the lines someone wrote for a slut in a porn flick and shattering them into a new kind of life, a life that is dazzling and sickening at once. I want to scream along, display myself in all my confused wanting, to be a little girl who is seen *and* heard.

The seventies were a time when the obscene was the last refuge of the sane. A bloated culture made by corporations paraded itself everywhere as common sense and sensual bliss at the same time. Collective political action had collapsed into a morass of "self" cultivation that blinded people to the extent of their oppression. Cities festered in anger, poverty, and debris that no normal person wanted to live around. So that left all the other people, the abnormals, to make anything they wanted out of the crap that was left lying around. Those people made hip-hop, punk rock; they made art of cellophane and dime-store kitsch. They made performances in which they braved the city streets for a year, or they found old stag movies and made them into art events by running them over and over again. Buildings were abandoned, and populations were left to shift for them- selves. The explosion of innovation that marked the art worlds of the early sixties had cooled and condensed into batches of new establishments, but there was another generation ready to take up the strategies that had been abandoned, an artistic generation for whom reaching for the scissors and glue was more natural than reaching for the paintbrush or the typewriter.

It's hard today to understand the unique valences of collaging—how different it was then. Now "cut" and "paste" are computer keyboard commands that carry no charge at all, since they are always accompanied by the possibility of the command "undo." Before the digital age, cutting always carried with it the knowledge of loss, to cut up and recombine entailed a leap of faith since the resulting thing might never be as good as the thing you destroyed to make it. But what about now, when every act of destruction can be erased as soon as it's enacted?

2. Fan

I first heard about Kathy Acker's work from a teacher. In 1980 I was an art major at Bard College, satisfying an English requirement by taking a tutorial with the poet Robert Kelly. I had said that I was going to be writing "performance scripts," but having forgotten that writing plays actually entailed sitting down and writing, I wasn't making much headway. One afternoon I found myself in front of Robert explaining an elaborate system I had worked out for a puppet show, whose script would change from performance to performance, because it would be composed of small sections that would be reconfigured by spinning a segmented wheel over and over again at the performance's beginning. While I had charted out several of the narrative snippets that would be grist for this chance operation, I hadn't bothered to actually write any of them. I had probably gotten the idea from making film loops with found footage in the previous years, but hadn't made the leap from found footage to found text. I was, in a word, winging it: a twenty-year-old with a lot of ideas culled from other artists but with very little of the work habits that might make those ideas anything other than vague possibilities. That didn't stop me from explaining those possibilities to Robert, who finally responded to my meanderings with an astute and patient suggestion: "There's a writer whose work I think you'll like: her name is Kathy Acker."

Even prior to college I was an art-world baby. When I was fourteen years old I would sneak out of my high school in order to hang around with the downtown avant-garde filmmakers and painters who were probably far more fascinated by my schoolgirl uniform than by any other aspect of whatever's called "me".[2]

Shortly after talking to Robert I was back in New York City and tracked down two books: *The Childlike Life of the Black Tarantula by the Black Tarantula* and *The Adult life of Toulouse Lautrec by Toulouse Lautrec*. The covers were confusing. Only by repeatedly checking the spine and the copyright page was I able to determine that these were Kathy Acker books. The editions are on my table in front of me right now. They are squat and simple in design, obviously the products of a small press. They reminded me of the artists' books I used to go downtown to buy at Printed Matter, and of the Grove Press edition of *My Secret Life by Anonymous*, a pornographic Edwardian memoir that my parents had on their living-room shelf, and that I used to sneak into my room and masturbate to.

To say I read Acker's books with growing enthusiasm would be an understatement. They were the first books in years that I read in the way I listened to favorite albums: over and over, until the pauses between songs were as much a part of the experience as the songs themselves. I read them like they were letters written to me. Why did I love those two small books? In part because they contained passages like this:

> "You're a raving maniac!!" I screech at the top of my lungs. "I believe artists can do everything! Artists can know all the joy and misery and terrifyingness and usefulness because artists don't have to suffer! Even though I can barely walk; I'm always in pain; I'm always hungry.

All I think about is sex. At night, nights, I lie alone in bed: I see the right leg of every sexy man I've ever seen on the street, the folds of cloth over and around the ooo ooo . . . I ache and I ache and I ache. I feel a big huge hole inside of my body. I see a man I like about to stick his cock in my hot pussy."[3]

Here was someone who wrote about artists and about fucking, two things I thought about a lot. Someone who had a middle-class New York upbringing like mine and who read porn and was willing themselves out of their family and into some new, different social configuration that meant escape and also meant the possibility of making things, of being around other people who made things. She induced in me a state that I can only refer to as cunt envy. The artists she wrote about were the ones whose work I had sneaked out of high school to look at, and she wrote with alternating sympathy and disdain about their money-grubbing, their tribal rituals, and glamorous poverties. Like the characters in her books, I too walked around New York looking to get a show and to get laid, hanging around the porn bookstores in Times Square fingering books like *The Gay Whores* while checking out the crotches of my fellow patrons.

Kathy Acker books placed the act of reading at their center. They made me think that my own reading wasn't useless, that it could be generative, that I could "find" text in the same way that I had found footage for my films or images in the old *National Geographics* I cut up to make cassette cases or postcards to send to my friends. I had read William Burroughs and Samuel Delaney years earlier; both had confounded me. It wasn't until reading Acker that I understood that other writers' narratives could be chopped up and reconfigured to suit my needs. While her books were formally familiar to me because of the art I'd seen grown up, the stories that they told and the images they contained were of those things I aspired to.

Throughout the seventies, while artists reinvented cities' failing industrial landscapes as new places for making work, gay men colonized those spaces as a sexual terrain, living out pornographers' fervid scenarios. Acker shows that the exultation of that freedom is only a prelude to further ambiguities. Her characters often escape the family, but like the singer in the Velvet Underground's *I'm Set Free* they often find they are ". . . set free to find a new illusion." Her strategy of fracturing and remaking culture presents writing as a way of moving through the world, one that never ceases. Stories don't conclude, they simply breed more stories.

I've often thought about why Acker's work has so much appeal for queer readers. In her literary world there are two groupings : family, which is the birthplace of the state, and friends, a confederation known variously as pirates, artists, whores. In part they are her version of Burroughs's Wild Boys. Her characters are engaged in one long escape from the family/state into the band, the tribe. For queers, the option of family is foreclosed, so the band is all we have left. To be marked by one's sexuality, indeed to be marked as sexual first and foremost is the fate that her characters offer themselves up to:

> "Sex is public: the streets made themselves for us to walk naked down them take out your cock and piss over me."[4]

It's belaboring an already overstated point to connect Acker's work with punk. After a while it was a liability for her to be saddled with the tag "punk writer" because it so narrowly defined her. It is useful to remember, however, how much punk was a music shaped by the art that proceeded it, art that was modest and homemade like fluxus, austere and repetitive like minimalism, or strategy-based like conceptualism. One of her earliest romantic involvements was with P. Adams Sitney, the leading theorist of New York's avant-garde film scene. As much as Acker's work is indebted to the cut-ups of Burroughs, it also resembled the found footage films of Bruce Conner, Ken Jacobs, and Peter Kubelka. Indeed, her heroines, questing for self-knowledge, could easily have stepped out of Maya Deren's *Meshes in the Afternoon*, a film where the female protagonist embarks on an ambiguous journey of self-definition/destruction. (Indeed, it might be interesting to study the varieties of Deren's influence on Acker, including her writings on Haiti.) In the early seventies the boundaries between the worlds of visual art, performance, and film were much more permeable than they are now. Artists crossed them easily, and passed ideas back and forth readily. In New York at least, much of what was later called punk was first identified as "art rock."

> I remember, when I was fifteen, Jack Smith telling me that what he most wanted to do was build a huge dome somewhere in North Africa. Whoever entered this dome would tell Jack his or her dreams and instantaneously Jack

would make a movie of this dream or series of dreams. Movie would be shown twenty-four hours a day.[5]

What marks Acker as an artist of her generation is the way she combined formal editing strategies that had previously been used to produce an effect of intellectual distance with content of overwhelming intimacy. This in part is the lesson she learned from Sade, but it is also present in much of Bruce Conner's work. It is also the technique of hip-hop: a record is in itself an utterly alienated and impersonal thing. The needle touches it and it plays. The best you can hope to do is to consume the music, like a reader consumes a book. But by disrupting the expected use of the record by replaying the bass line over and over, by changing the sound levels, by extention and compression the record is made back into a musical instrument. Acker remakes the possibilities of text into her instruments, by treating text as a thing, a material to be sliced up and pushed around. She skins the characters and narratives she finds and constructs her own suit out of them.

In a way, reading Acker regresses me, bringing me back to the desire to be in the land of make-believe. This is, of course, the same effect as pornography, a form that makes a place for us to escape into. Porn novels are like fairy tales before Perrault got his hands on them: episodic, morally ambiguous, repetitive, more interested in the arrangement of the characters than in emotional depth or forward narrative motion. For the most part they were written anonymously by people who had to churn them out on a schedule. (In the late seventies I went to a porn publisher looking for work drawing covers of the books. What I remember vividly of that visit is a row of rumpled men seated at typewriters turning out the novels. Each typewriter was being fed paper off of large rollers; I presume the hacks were being paid by the inch.)

In the end the puppet show I tortured Robert with never got made, and the tutorial is marked "incomplete" on my transcripts to this day. But in pointing me to Acker, Robert gave me something that every artist needs: an ideal audience, a person I could treat like a confidant and an ally even though she didn't have the slightest idea that I was alive. I wanted to turn my work into a dialogue, to insert it into a larger discussion, to be part of the world of artists I had admired growing up. Encountering Kathy Acker's work made me feel I could do that. In the twenty-five years since his suggestion I've had occasion to thank Robert mentally for uttering that sentence. I'm doing so again now.

3. Low

In 1990 I finally worked with Kathy. It is more accurate to say that I purchased her attention. I had been living in San Francisco since 1984 and over the years had gotten to know a few people who were also friends of hers. Because of that I had also come to think of myself as some part of the tribe that I had been so entranced with growing up. Back in New York, the cluttered broken collage aesthetic of the late seventies and early eighties had yielded to work that revelled in machined polish and theoretical gloss. The new work claimed to expose the hollowness of commodity culture and paradoxically produced fabulously successful commodities. For the first time it was possible to make a decent living as an American artist: to appear in magazines, to purchase a country home, to approximate chic. I was preparing my first solo show in New York and persuaded my gallery there to hire Kathy to write a catalogue essay. Once she agreed, we met. I showed her a bunch of slides of my work, talked to her in the standard way I talked to everyone about what I thought I was doing, and then she interviewed me. Did I have any recurring dreams? What was my childhood like? I told her about growing up on the West Side in New York City, with parents of differing races, about my younger sister, about being an art nerd in high school. Our talk was hedged by my over-eagerness and her diffidence.

Months later she sent in her text for the book. When I read it I was puzzled. I thought the parts of it that looked more like fiction were somewhat successful, and the parts that were written as traditional art criticism, with their references to the mythic and to American optimism, were labored and off the mark. More than that, I wasn't seeing myself in the story. There wasn't even anything gay in it. I wanted to tell her that it was okay, she didn't have to write an "art essay," all that she had to do was transform me, to make me over into one of the desperate, smart, horny outsiders who populated her books; all she had to do was to understand through looking at my work that I had read her work and I had understood. In 1990 I was so impatient to get through that door that I tried cutting the line. I wanted Kathy to take me seriously, for me to reside in her thoughts in a way that would echo how she resided in mine. The book that resulted from our collaboration is a slim hardback similar in format to the earliest of the books of hers I had bought in art school, except that this one was full of color reproductions of things I had made.

Chain-store chain-smoke
I consume you all
Chain-gang chain-mail
I don't think at all

Oh bondage up yours
Oh bondage no more
Oh bondage up yours
Oh bondage no more

It doesn't work that way. Even though queers can choose their tribe, artists can't chose their clan, the clutch of people who will see their work for what it is and value it, any more than one can choose the person who's going to fall in love with you. Artistic communication is more complex than simple identification. My own convictions about the similarities in what we did was no guarantee that she would see it that way. I hadn't reckoned on the one thing that we perhaps had most in common: the highly cultivated narcissism we each used to make our work.

At the time, the project felt like a misfire. But one of its results was that we became friends. Soon after she moved to San Francisco, and I saw her a great deal more. She came to the Thanksgiving dinner my boyfriend and I hosted. I read her new books as they were published, with varying degrees of enthusiasm. We both began to teach at the San Francisco Art Institute and chatted in its coffee shop about various tattooists. As a friend she was charming, flirtatious, vital, and infuriating by turns. I think it was a marker of how far our friendship had progressed that I finally saw the ugly side of her competitiveness: at one point we had both been asked to be guest lecturers at a school in the East Bay. She seemed uncomfortable sharing the spotlight. During my talk she publicly corrected me with a tiny flourish on meanness. That day I gave her a drawing; she barely acknowledged it. By the mid-nineties, we saw little of each other. I moved back to New York, hearing shortly after about her illness.

4. Heard

I started this essay with the charge to talk about the relation between Kathy Acker's work and that of visual artists, in part through a history of our collaboration on *Low*. But that's an awfully simple word, collaboration, masking as it does the cross-currents of influence, erasure, devotion, and competition. Instead I'd rather substitute two questions: What did she make of my work? What did I make of hers?

After I learned that Kathy died, I picked up a copy of *Low* and reread her essay. In it she wrote about innocence, hysteria, American optimism, Hansel and Gretel, and William Blake. At the end is a transfiguration of one of the dreams she had asked me about: a dream in which I wander around in the American Museum of Natural History until the dioramas begin to fill with water, the animals moving inside the murk, the glass shattering, leaving me floundering waist-deep in sharks. I see now how she captured much of what I have become as an artist. Her writing was more predictive than descriptive. When it was written I valued cleverness, the operation of my own mind through my work. I wanted my ideas taken seriously as part of an art-historical argument. In time I've come to value more and more the emotional life of my work. I care less about ideological positions and more about inhabiting the moment of creation, manifesting my pleasures through making. I used to wish to be thought of as adult. Now my work seems more and more to revolve around the images and stories of childhood, my own and others.

In 1998 I had a small, two-room exhibition that I titled "Feeder2 and corollary." In the first room of the show I built a cabin, seven by seven by ten feet, out of steel and gingerbread. In the second room were four things: two prints of a blurred photograph of a snow-covered cabin, a vitrine containing a six-pack of bottles of Brer Rabbit brand Molasses, and a one-hour videotape in which I am fed over and over again by another man.

The Cabin ("Feeder2") was large enough for adults to enter if they crouched under the doorway. Children ran right in. The smell of gingerbread, enticing in the gallery, turned thick and buttery once you got inside the house. Its temptation proved too much for many people, who broke off chunks of the piece to nibble on. The first "Feeder" was a piece I had made for the show in 1990, a large steel cage with a waist-high slot. In her essay Kathy turned it into the "animal-restraining cage" that the witch locks Hansel into. "Feeder's" shape is that of the witch's cookie hut, but also that of the prototypical American Log cabin, the one Abe Lincoln was born in, or Uncle Tom's.

You need molasses to make gingerbread, but the bottles in the back room are linked together like a six-pack of soda pop. On the video, a shirtless black man encourages? forces? me to eat donuts, pizza, sandwiches, watermelon, chocolate. He pours milk down my throat. Is this care, subservience, slavery, abuse? Am I being nourished, punished, infantilized, fucked, reduced to a hole to be filled? After seeing the tape, one had to pass the gingerbread house again to exit. I like to think that the show began to ask the question: What happens when we get what we want? Is this what bliss looks like, smells like?

It's a question Kathy taught me to ask.

I like to think that this is how I finally returned the volley of her writing about me: I used her thoughts and images as a blueprint for my liberation and as a brick to smash the illusion that that liberation embodied. It had never occurred to me to look at the Hansel and Gretel story, to inhabit it, until I reread that essay and let those words work on me. Ultimately that is how artists work together, by allowing each other's ideas to work on them. I no longer believe that I can find safety in a three-minute punk squall. But I can add my voice to that noise, I can make something that echoes that call. I'm sorry that Kathy was never able to see the ways in which I tried to make use of what she gave me. Sometimes that's how collaboration happens: blindly, in halting fragments that spill through time.

I had told her about a dream and she made a book out of it, a book that also embodied the dream I hadn't dared to tell her about—the dream of belonging. Her writing is partially the fulfillment of Jack Smith's plan: the arena where dreams are confessed and made into gigantic art, to be seen round the clock: the palace of wonder.

I hope that this essay contains the monstrousness of my desire. It is part of my story that all I've ever wanted to be is a character in a book. I've come to know through experience that that isn't as nice a feeling as I thought it would be and also that getting one's wishes fulfilled carries with it a responsibility to a work whose final form can barely be guessed at.

> Thrash me crash me
> Beat me till I fall
> I wanna be a victim
> For you all

Oh bondage up yours
Oh bondage no more
Oh bondage up yours
Oh bondage no more

Repeat first verse

Notes

1. Lyrics by Poly Styrene, copyright 1978 Phantom Publishing Ltd.
2. Kathy Acker, "Critical Languages," in *Bodies of Work* (London, Serpent's Tail, 1997, p. 83.
3. *The Adult Life of Toulouse Lautrec by Henri Toulouse Lautrec* (New York, TVRT Press,1975), p. 6.
4. *Great Expectations* (New York, Open Book/Station Hill Press, 1982), p. 113.
5. "Critical Languages," p. 83.

Seventeen Paragraphs on Kathy Acker

Leslie Dick

1. When I knew her, in London, Kathy had two lovebirds called Eulalie and Legba, after Voodoo gods. She decorated their large cage with many mirrors and other trinkets, and she made faces and cooed at them at frequent intervals. Sometimes I felt she imagined herself to be a lovebird, with her odd face elongated into a parrot's beak. She spoke to her birds in their language, and was delighted by their cooing replies. When eventually one of the birds became ill, she found it unbearable to watch the bird die. In the end, she took the expiring lovebird and carried him outside her flat, to place him gently on the ground under a bit of shrubbery. She told me that after turning away tearfully, she saw a cat wandering around, and she was convinced Legba had met his end in the cat's jaws. This scene gave her a certain ironic satisfaction: when things got rough, it confirmed her deeply held view that everything was both terrible and meaningless, and this confirmation seemed almost to strike a balance; it made the spinning world steady for a time. Her sense of dark comedy came through, at the very same time as a practical acknowledgement that this was the limit, she wasn't going to go through this again, so could I please come in my car to drive her and the surviving lovebird across London to Mile End, so she could give the bereft bird back to the man she'd bought them from originally, and be rid of the whole thing. It was a long drive, in traffic, and on the way back we stopped for a swim in a big municipal swimming bath, its water heavy with chemicals suffusing the damp air. We rented our bathing suits from the Borough, and afterwards our skin reeked of chlorine.

2. David Antin, in conversation some years ago, described how he used to tell his students at University of California, San Diego, that they didn't have to live the things they wanted to write, instead they could go to a book, an encyclopedia, a

newspaper, and copy it out. Once you get rid of the idea of the original artwork created by the unique artist, you are left with subjectivity, sexuality (subjectivity's sister), and the copy. Kathy Acker copied out classics, rewriting *Don Quixote* and *Great Expectations*. She copied out, wrote and rewrote porn, later she copied out schlock bestsellers like *The Carpetbaggers* and stylish sci-fi like *Neuromancer*, and she also copied out her own life, in a relentlessly repetitive process of transcription that called every received idea about literary value into question. Everything she wrote raised questions of truth and fiction, property and theft, and the relations of power that determine value and meaning.

3. Kathy wrote four pages a day, in a notebook, no matter what. I remember coming to see her and Kathy opening the door of her flat and saying, Just a moment, I just have to finish this, and then—in what seemed almost to be a demonstration, or a performance, of writing—she took her fountain pen to slowly trace the letters of the last words, to fill the last line of the fourth page.

4. A key context for Kathy Acker's work in the 1970s and early 80s was the New York art scene—a context in which performance art, acts of sexual and formal transgression, and misappropriation of the found object (or text) were crucial to a number of contemporaries. Such a context includes many women artists and writers, such as Patti Smith, Jenny Holzer, Barbara Kruger, Lynne Tillman, Laurie Anderson, Diamanda Galas, and various punk rockers. Other performance artists were also significant, such as Carolee Schneemann and Richard Foreman, both of whose work foregrounds the problematic relationship of language and the body, although in very different ways. Arguably, Kathy Acker took bits and pieces from contemporary art and performance practice—such as using a repetitive rule-based system for producing work (Acker rewrote her texts eight times: once for sound, once for meaning, once for "beauty," once for structure, once in the mirror for performativity, etc), or the practice of refunctioning "found texts," copying and re-contextualizing fragments of the real world, recycling chunks of the already used.

5. To a great extent, the gods of this New York scene, looming over all of us, were two gay men: William S. Burroughs and Andy Warhol, the ultimate copycat. Any woman artist necessarily took up an oblique, a displaced relation to these heroes, as the insistence on issues of feminism, and/or a female body pushes everything

into a different register. Later, other ideas circulating out of situationist thinking, of the city as a site for drifting subjectivity, and the artwork as a place where already existing meanings can be diverted and reconfigured, were also crucial. *"Détournement"* translates as misappropriation (of funds), hijacking (of a plane or a ship), or diversion (of a road or river). The idea that meaning can itself be hijacked in an act of what used to be known as "cultural terrorism" is central to the period I remember.

6. It was Jane Weinstock who introduced Kathy to me, in New York, in December 1982. We were in the street, on the corner, and we talked for a minute or two. Kathy seemed both shy and outrageous in her self-presentation. It was on Jane's bookshelves that I first encountered Kathy's work. I was starting to write, and it made an enormous impact on me, along the lines of: "if she can do that, then I can do this." Read alongside Lynne Tillman's work, and other women writers published in Anne Turyn's *Top Stories* magazine, *Between C & D*, *Bomb*, and in *Semiotext(e)*, this writing literally opened up a space of possibility; like punk rock, it smashed things wide open and left room for other people (me) to do very different things. In my work, I wasn't so interested in appropriation as a literary strategy, but the sense that "everything is permitted," which Kathy's (and others') writing produced, seems almost to have been a precondition for pursuing my own writing project, that is, articulating the awkward territory where theory and everyday life intersect. It wasn't until I was going out with Peter Wollen, later, that I got to know Kathy as a friend, in London. She would introduce Peter and me as "my parents," which sometimes sounded like "my parrots," and sometimes more like "my pirates." I remember sitting with her on a sofa at a party and looking into her face, with its harsh makeup and amazing punk hair, peroxide blonde then with brown burn marks on it as if it had been seared with a branding iron, and recognizing this spectacle as a mask that she peered out from behind, or within, oddly like a little girl.

7. Kathy Acker's readings, her self-presentation (both live and photographic) through clothes, hair, exposure of skin, tattoos, etc., her presence on the covers of her books, all worked explicitly to place her body as an obstacle, a threat and a promise, mediating between the reader and the text. Her small self-published books were like LPs, her readings were always a performance, and the sheer

physical presence of her body and the sound of her voice were central to her project. Writing sex as Kathy does also works to bring the reader back to her body in a way no other literary strategy quite does. At that time, the late seventies and early eighties, debate around pornography and feminism, pleasure and danger, was heated; yet, the paradoxical proposition that a specific body was always implicated in the construction of identity (and yet did not restrict the possible identifications and fantasies that that very body might enjoy) was itself a feminist idea. Kathy Acker took some of these ideas and played them out, like a card game, to display their operation, to make them work.

8. Kathy spent one Christmas Day walking the streets of London all alone, in the cold and dark, looking into brightly lit windows, in a fervent re-enactment of the Little Match Girl. She was in a perpetual state of suffering, with excruciating pelvic inflammatory disease that came and went, or romantic distress: whoever she was with always seemed to be treating her unkind. I remember her elucidating a crucial distinction: "I'll be his slave, but I won't be his *dog*." Of course I thought being his slave wasn't necessarily such a great idea either, but I was always much more cautious in that department than Kathy.

9. Once Kathy was asked to give a reading at Readers and Writers, the radical bookstore in Camden Town, and she told them she'd do it if I could read, too. It was at that reading that Pete Ayrton, who was just starting Serpent's Tail, came up to me and said, I hear you have a novel, we'd like to see it. This was my first book, the one that was rejected by every other publisher in England. Serpent's Tail published it, and later it was Kathy who gave a copy of that book to Amy Scholder when she came through London, when Amy asked if there was anything good and new to read. Amy took it back to City Lights, and they published it in the US, and still do. Kathy's generosity to unpublished writers was legendary. In the end we fell out. It was inevitable. Nevertheless I won't forget her generosity to me.

10. The relation of words and things, writing and life, is a relation that never quite matches—it's asymptotic, as Lacan says, the *je* and the *moi* (asymptotic always sounds to me like asymptomatic, like chlamydia, but anyway)—and it is in that gap between words and things, in that rupture, that desire lies. Put bluntly, need is a material reality, like hunger or love, and demand the speech act that repeats that

need in words. In the difference between them, a difference that can never be evaded, given the infinitely incommensurable mismatch of things and words, bodies and ideas, in the difference between need and demand, in that impossible subtraction, desire comes into being. Kathy Acker's work is located there.

11. Kathy got at that space partly by refusing the distinction between art and life, words and things, by mixing it up to the point where every text undoes the proper and proprietary boundaries between the author and her very own text. This presumed author, singular in its authority, dissolves in Kathy's writing, vanishing into a rapid sequence of possible others, while the text violates every literary rule of etiquette regarding the artist's personal history, her privacy, sexuality, and bodily functions. Kathy shoved it all together: great literature, pornography, schlock novels, movies, poetry of many lands, science fiction, detective stories, and other genres. She put these and more into her writing alongside and within her own real life stories—stories of heartbreak, sexual longing, physical and psychic pain and ecstasy. In the collision, in this mix, the space between words and things starts to open up, to come apart, to break down into something else: into a text of desire, always marked by the shadow of the lost object.

12. Freud says the fetish serves two purposes: it both covers up the absence, effacing the loss ('course, he claims what's lost is the mother's penis, which never existed anyway, but we are under no obligation to insist on that point, here, the lost object could be the mother herself). Anyway, the fetish both covers up the absence, the loss, denying it, and at the very same moment it serves as a memorial to the loss; it is like a stone set up to mark the grave, or the wound, a marker for memory. In replacing the lost object, the fetish remembers the very absence it conceals.[1]

13. I like the idea of the fetish as a signifier that swings both ways, insistently repeating the loss while at the same time denying it, covering it up. And in some sense this is what language does all the time; it's a substitute, replacing the object (and thus filling the gap) and at the same time marking the gap, pointing to the absence of the object. The material world is both proposed (in imagination) and denied by language, in an amazing process where imagined experience is both evoked and crossed out endlessly.

14. Kathy's writing cancels itself out all the time, as one thing supersedes another, taking its place in a sequence that refuses to build. As Emily Apter said to me, Kathy takes the *Bildung* out of the *Bildungsroman*—she takes the goal orientation out of *Great Expectations*, the aging out of the coming-of-age narrative. Instead Kathy freezes the narrative momentum, struggling to replace the relentless sequencing of narrative development with a Steinian present—and all the growing up that is implied in that *Bildung* story falls apart, regresses, comes undone, so that innocence, in all its depravity, its abject vulnerability, can emerge.

15. Kathy's work proposes a childlike poly-identity, which has a psychological resonance as well as political and literary dimensions. Like a recalcitrant child, she sets to work to break every writerly rule: the first and most fundamental rule of originality is exploded in a relentless practice of plagiarism; the idea of continuity—of authorial voice, of character, of narrative progression—is shattered. Most particularly, any kind of gender continuity is continually called into question, while genres are thrown together to disrupt and disturb and disorientate any reading that settles into a comfortable pattern for more than a moment or two. Kathy's writing refuses narrative momentum: there's no suspense, no temporal logic, above all, no resolution. No closure. (*Great Expectations* ends: "Dear mother,—" and then the void. It ends at a beginning, it leaves me hanging, it lets me know to whom this writing is addressed.) She inserts drawings, maps, diagrams, other languages, humorous asides, to break things up, to break the reading up, to get at the anguish of a text of desire. I believe Kathy saw existing books as objects in the world, sculptural, three dimensional, material things, glued and sewn together out of paper and board, and by cutting into them, rewriting them, making them work against each other, she was playing with and playing out the differences between words and things.

16. Rereading, I'm struck by the set-ups, the opening moves: Kathy introduces some version of herself as character, she gives the character's situation, the setting, and then this is quickly abandoned, without a backward glance. Whatever scenario is proposed is almost immediately dismantled, as if boredom is always lurking and must be outrun, using device after device to undo cumulative narrative logic. Or possibly it's not boredom, it's just literary convention in all its rigor, which must somehow be outmaneuvered in this way. It's like a machine, it's automatic, the way

the reader takes almost anything you give to turn it into a story, with a beginning, middle, and an end. But Kathy won't allow it, which is one reason why her work is so disturbing: it's not just the violence, the self-mutilation, the incest, the pain. It's that her text won't let us read in the way we automatically like to do.

17. Kathy's method of folding in radically opposed texts, with no boundaries between them, produces a writing where each text works to call into question the underlying (structural) assumptions of the next, to the point where porn is interrogated by theory, mystery stories are intersected by poetry. She uses already existing texts against each other: by merging Wedekind's "Lulu" and Shaw's "Eliza Doolittle," for example, she demonstrates how they are two sides of the same coin: except Eliza's in a romantic comedy, so she's on her way up the social ladder, whereas Lulu will end up in the gutter. They are both pictures of innocence, and therefore, in Kathy's world, destined sooner or later to be sold as prostitutes. Power is materialized in proper language (the Queen's English in what Eliza learns to speak—"the rain in Spain," and so forth) and the comedy of *Pygmalion* (or *My Fair Lady*) is turned inside out, to expose its dark lining, Lulu's anguish, her passivity and her violent death. In Kathy's work, no one genre or mode of representation remains stable for long enough to find its feet, to dominate. In the landscape mapped out in her writing, the interzone between words and things, she uses every literary structure and trope, emphasizing poetic structures, translation, rhythm and sound, to insist on the materiality of the signifier—because if language is a thing in the world, then it cannot ever be merely transparent, a stepping-stone to meaning. Instead, it is language itself which dominates, creating a strange equilibrium, that is, a condition where opposing forces cancel each other out, leaving only words, in a terrible present, in all their materiality.

Notes

1. Sigmund Freud, "Fetishism", *Standard Edition* vol. XXI (1927), pp. 149–159.

Contributors

Nayland Blake is represented by Matthew Marks Gallery in New York City, and is exhibited widely in the US and abroad. He teaches at the International Center for Photography—Bard Graduate Program.

Leslie Dick teaches at California Institute of the Arts, and is the author of *The Skull of Charlotte Corday*, *Kicking*, and *Without Falling*.

Robert Glück teaches at San Francisco State University and is the author of *Denny Smith Stories*, *Margery Kempe*, *Jack the Modernist*, and other books.

Carla Harryman teaches at Wayne State University, and is the author of *Baby*, *Gardener of Stars*, *There Never Was a Rose without a Thorn*, and other books.

Laurence A. Rickels teaches at the University of California, Santa Barbara, and is the author of *Aberrations of Mourning*, *The Case of California*, *Nazi Psychoanalysis*, and *The Vampire Lectures*. Two new books, *The Autobiography of Art Cinema* and *Devil Father Mine*, are forthcoming.

Avital Ronell teaches at New York University, The European Graduate School and Paris VIII. She is the author of many books including *The Test Drive*, *Stupidity*, and *Crack Wars: Literature, Addiction, Mania*.

Amy Scholder is the US Publisher of Verso. She has also published books with Serpent's Tail, City Lights Books, Grove Press, New Museum of Contemporary Art, and elsewhere.

Barrett Watten teaches at Wayne State University and is the author of *The Constructivist Moment: From Material Text to Cultural Poetics, Progress/Under Erasure,* and *Frame (1971–1990),* among other books.

Peter Wollen is the author of many books including *Signs and Meaning in the Cinema, Raiding the Icebox: Reflections on Twentieth-Century Culture, Paris Hollywood: Writings on Film,* and *Paris Manhattan: Writing on Art.*

Index

Printed in the United States
by Baker & Taylor Publisher Services